Tips and Traps When Buying a Condo, Co-op, or Townhouse

Other McGraw-Hill Books by Robert Irwin

Tips and Traps When Buying a Condo, Co-op, or Townhouse

Robert Irwin

McGraw-Hill

New York San Francisco Washington, D.C. Auckland Bogotá
Caracas Lisbon London Madrid Mexico City Milan
Montreal New Delhi San Juan Singapore
Sydney Tokyo Toronto

Library of Congress Cataloging-in-Publication Data

Irwin, Robert.
    Tips and traps when buying a condo, co-op, or townhouse / Robert Irwin.
        p.   cm.
    Includes index.
    ISBN 0-07-134848-4
    1. House buying.   2. Condominiums.   3. Apartment houses, Cooperative.   4. Row houses.   5. Real estate business.   I. Title.
    HD1379.I669   1999
    643'.12—dc21   99-16831
                                                                         CIP

McGraw-Hill

*A Division of The **McGraw·Hill** Companies*

        4 5 6 7 8 9 0   DOC/DOC   0 9 8 7 6 5 4 3 2

ISBN 0-07-134848-4

It was set in Baskerville per the BSF TTS design by Joanne Morbit of the Professional Book Group's composition unit, Hightstown, N.J.

Printed and bound by R. R. Donnelley & Sons Company.

McGraw-Hill books are available at special quantity discounts to use as premiums and sales promotions, or for use in corporate training programs. For more information, please write to the Director of Special Sales, McGraw-Hill, Professional Publishing, Two Penn Plaza, New York, NY 10121-2298. Or contact your local bookstore.

This book contains the author's opinions. Some material in this book may be affected by changes in the law (or changes in interpretations of the law) or changes in market conditions since the manuscript was prepared. Therefore, the accuracy and completeness of the information contained in this book and the opinions based on it cannot be guaranteed. Neither the author nor the publisher is engaged in rendering investment, legal, tax, accounting, or other similar professional services. If these services are required, the reader should obtain them from a competent professional.

 This book is printed on recycled, acid-free paper containing a minimum of 50% recycled, de-inked fiber.

Contents

6. Beware the Architectural Committee! **53**

7. Special Tips and Traps When Buying a Condo **65**

8. Special Tips and Traps When Buying a Townhouse **75**

Appendix: When an Owner Defies the Board   **175**

Preface

Why a book on just condos, townhouses, and co-ops? Are they so different from single-family detached homes?

Indeed they are! They are a horse of an entirely different color. If you're buying a condo, townhouse, or co-op, don't make the BIG mistake of thinking it's just like any other kind of residential real estate—it's not!

When I first bought into a shared-ownership development, I was completely unprepared for what subsequently happened. I wanted to add-on to my unit. No way would the board allow it. Then I got an increase in my monthly assessment. At first I was furious, so angry that I eventually ran for the board in order to make changes, and I was elected! Then I developed a different perspective.

Being on the board, I wanted to protect the whole neighborhood. I wanted to preserve the lifestyle of the development. I wanted to be sure the overall homogeneous appearance didn't turn into a patchwork of different colors and styles. I wanted strict rules and financial security for the common good. I wanted to maintain and enhance the development's value. In essence I changed from "me" to "them."

I've enjoyed living in shared-ownership housing and being on many boards over the years. And I think that the vast majority of other owners have enjoyed their ownership as well. However, a condo, townhouse, or co-op is not for everyone. If it's not for you, jumping in can be a colossal financial and emotional disaster.

That's why I wrote this book—to let you look before you leap. There are many bonuses as well as many pitfalls to shared-ownership developments. I've tried to explain them all here. With this book you should be able to clearly see what you're getting into, whether it's something you want...or not.

Remember, don't buy a condo, townhouse, or co-op because it's cheaper or close to where you want to live or because somebody said it's a good deal. Buy it because you truly understand what you're getting yourself into...and because you really like what you see.

Robert Irwin

Acknowledgments

Many thanks to property manager extraordinaire Barbara Mintz for her help in clearly defining the technical definitions of condo and townhouse as well as the overall checking of the manuscript for loose ends. Also, grateful thanks to David Ganz, Esq., of Ganz, Hollinger and Towe (New York City) for reminding me of the many technical aspects of co-op ownership. And a special thanks to all those managers, board members, and property owners who shared their experiences, insights, and complaints—all of which made this book possible.

1

What Sharing Ownership Will Mean to You

Buying a condo, townhouse, or co-op is quite different from purchasing a single-family home. It's much more.

In a way, it's like marrying into a family. You hope that the attachment will result in meeting warm, wonderful people with whom you can spend many enjoyable hours. When you buy a condo, townhouse, or co-op, you're joining another group of owners in sharing common areas. You may look forward to partaking in amenities such as a swimming pool, spa, and tennis court, or to sharing picnics, barbecues, and other social events. Or, if you want, you may anticipate that you will be left alone to "do you own thing" without interference from others.

It could all come to pass as you hope.

Or your dreams could turn into nightmares. You could find that you've married into a dysfunctional family. Other owners could pester you with what you consider minor complaints. An intransigent homeowners organization could prevent you from doing simple things such as painting your front door a different color. You could find your life in the condo, townhouse, or co-op a living hell, so bad that you'll want to sell immediately, even at a loss.

Of course, things rarely get that bad. But they could *if* you purchase unwisely. That's what we're going to try to prevent in this book.

Here we will examine condos, townhouses, and co-ops with an eye toward discovering whether they are well worth your making the purchase or whether they are a ticking time bomb that you should

1

stay away from at all costs. We'll see what makes one development super while making another a poor investment. Overall, we'll come to understand this thing called "shared ownership" and see whether it's something you will or won't like.

Who Should Read This Book?

This book is designed for you if:

- You're considering the first-time purchase of a condo, townhouse, or co-op.
- You've already owned one of the above, had a bad experience, and want to find out how to be sure that next time it will be better.
- You've owned one of the above, had a good experience, and want to duplicate it.
- You're simply curious to learn more about shared ownership developments.

What Are Condos, Townhouses, and Co-ops?

Before proceeding, let's be sure we understand our terms:

Condominium Put most simply, you buy an airspace, like an apartment. You *own* the inside walls, floors, and ceilings. Everything else–including the outside walls, roof, walkways, driveways, swimming pool, and spa–you share with others.

Townhouse As with a condo, you own the inside and sometimes the ground below. The difference is that you don't have someone living above or below you. You still share walls, roads, recreational facilities, and so on with others.

Co-op You rent an apartment from a corporation in which you have ownership, as evidenced by shares of stock.

Of course, these are quick definitions. They will be expanded in later chapters on each of the different types of ownership. For now, however, let's get on with seeing what you should question before you buy.

2

How to Evaluate a Condo, Townhouse, or Co-op

I'm sure you've heard the adage that shared ownership units are the last to increase in value when times are good and the first to fall when times are bad. Perhaps you're wondering about the future. If you buy, will you have trouble reselling? Will you get your money out? Will you make a profit or have to accept a loss?

The trouble with adages is that they generalize at best and oversimplify at worst. Both are the case here. Well-located and well-designed shared units go up in price just as rapidly as single-family homes. And they hold (or lose) their value just as well when hard times hit. On the other hand, shared units that aren't so well located or well designed tend to go up slower and go down faster than many single-family homes. The key, of course, is to find a unit that's well located and well designed. That's what we'll cover in this chapter.

It's Still the Location

Everyone knows (or should know) by now that the most important factor influencing price in real estate is location. This is doubly true for shared ownership dwellings, because you're concerned not only with the overall location of the development but with the location of the unit itself within the development.

The Location of the Development

As with single-family homes, you want to buy into a property that has best possible location. This includes all of the following:

- Close to good schools (usually the number-one priority in terms of having good resale potential)

- In a low-crime area

- Close to a good residential "anchor" such as a beach or lake, downtown district, or desirable suburban location

- In a sharp-looking *residential* setting with a good mix of housing (single family as well as shared ownership)

- Easy access to freeways, mass transit, and airports so you can quickly get to a variety of employment opportunities

- Close to shopping and recreation

If you're using an agent, show him or her the above list and expect a chuckle, because you will have described the best area in town. The problem, of course, may be that it is very pricey, perhaps too expensive for your pocketbook. In that case, try to find an area with as many of the above features as possible. The list is from top to bottom in terms of priorities.

TIP

You should be able to get information on all the above from any broker or agent. Also check local chambers of commerce, police departments, and school districts. Much of the information can be obtained online using your computer. (Chambers of commerce, police departments, and schools often have their own Web sites.) Two good services for information are www.dataquick.com (for information on schools, crime, and more) and www.schools.com.

TRAP

Beware of a development that is situated in "apartment city." In other words, the whole area is nothing but shared unit developments and apartment buildings. This means a much higher population density over single-family neighborhoods—a serious detracting feature to any future buyers.

The "Curb Appeal" Factor

As with any real estate, how the property looks the first time you pull up to it is important. A good-looking shared ownership development will have an appealing front. It need not look like the Taj Mahal, but it should be imposing in a residential sort of way. The appearance should say that this is a respectable area where people are safe and free to have "quiet enjoyment" of their home. In other words, it's a place you would want to live.

More exclusive areas may have a gate with a guard (or a doorman or keyed entrance) to help with privacy and security. Ideally, the shared community is surrounded by single-family homes with no commercial development immediately nearby. (The exception could be a downtown urban setting.)

TRAP

Having a gas station or quick-service store on the corner may be convenient, but it will knock down the value of the location. You want the commercial development to be at least a couple of blocks away. This goes for shopping centers (with their lit parking lots and heavy traffic) as well.

The Location of the Unit Within the Development

Assuming that the development you are considering passes muster, the next concern should be the unit within the development itself.

It's important to remember that not all locations within a development are equally valued.

For example, I was recently considering a development that was noted for its vista of mountains off to the east. Indeed, the view from those units facing eastward was impressive. However, the view from those units facing north, west, and south left much to be desired. In other words, the view, on which the reputation of the development was based, was available only from about a quarter of the units. If I were buying one of those, I would indeed be getting my money's worth. However, if I bought one of the other units, I'd end up paying a premium, because of the reputation of the development, but not get the view. This means more money when I bought, and a harder time convincing a future buyer when I wanted to resell.

TIP

When buying into a development that has a special feature, such as a view, be sure your unit has access to that feature.

Other concerns about location within the development can be more obvious. For example, you don't want to buy the unit that's located next to the garbage dumpsters. Some, however, are less obvious. We'll consider a few below.

Does It Have an Acceptable View?

We've already discussed view as a major feature, such as a view of the mountains or the ocean or a river. But there are less esoteric concerns. Does the unit face a tree-lined greenbelt, or does it have a view of the driveway? While most of us like looking at trees, we don't have much fondness for watching asphalt.

The worst development I ever saw had lovely units on the outside facing greenbelts. However, the inside units were surrounded on all four sides by driveways. No matter where you looked, there were cars going by or parked. Not a pleasant place.

TRAP

Beware the inside view. In some larger developments, the inside units simply face other units over a small courtyard. While it's true that the inside units typically will sell for less, it's also true that it's hard to find a buyer for them at a reasonable price when it comes time for you to resell.

Is It Noisy?

Most homeowners don't want a lot of noise. They want "quiet enjoyment" of their property. Yet noise in any shared development, with so many people living together, is bound to be a concern. Here are some particularly noisy areas to avoid:

- The unit faces a busy street.

- The unit is near a swimming pool or recreational center. (These units are often promoted as prime because of their proximity to amenities. But the noise usually more than outweighs any advantage of being able to walk right over.)

- It is a corner unit with windows on two streets.

- The unit faces a school, shopping center, or other facility that attracts lots of people.

- The unit is near garages or carports where cars are constantly coming and going.

- The unit is near noisy neighbors.

TIP

Check out the neighbors before you buy. You can talk to them and others and get some idea of how quiet or noisy the unit you are considering is. Even better, come by at night or dinnertime a couple of days during the week to see for yourself.

TRAP

Generally speaking, neighbors with kids are noisier than neighbors without. This can be particularly the case for teenagers who play loud music and throw frequent parties.

Is the Density Livable?

Density refers to the number of people who live within the development (and around it). Lower density is always more desirable. The fewer owners who are crowded together in an area, the more each of them will enjoy the property. There will be less noise, you will find it less crowded when you use the swimming pool or tennis court, and you'll find that you see your neighbors less often, which is something most people appreciate.

TIP

Always look for the lowest-density development. That means the fewest units spread farthest apart.

The biggest single benefit that townhouses have over condominiums, indeed, is the lower density. With condos the units are literally one on top of the other. With townhouses, they are only side by side. As a rule, all else being equal, townhouses are always pricier and more desired than condos.

I'm often asked about the proper density. In other words, how many people per square foot? Unfortunately, there's no clear answer. Each development is different and a lot depends on how the developer put it together. I've seen condo and co-op units that somehow managed to have small but lovely patios that gave them the feeling of spaciousness. On the other hand, I've seen large townhouses that looked uncomfortably squeezed together.

Density is a judgment call. I usually try standing on the street next to the unit (or nearby the entrance) at dinnertime (when most people are home) simply to get a feeling for how close everyone is. If it feels good, then it probably isn't too dense. If I feel cooped up, then it's probably too dense.

TRAP

A quick way to check for density within a development is to look for parking spaces. Every owner will have at least one (possibly two or more) parking spaces in a garage, carport, or open area. If it seems like everywhere you turn outside the unit there are parking spaces, then it's probably too dense. On the other hand, it's a good sign if the parking is gracefully built into the design of the development.

Is It Safe?

Unfortunately, we live in an age when crime is a major concern for homeowners. While overall safety within a development may be high, some units may be safer than others. For example, a few units in a development may be less safe because they're outside the perimeter fence, or face the public street directly, or even are close to the entrance. In a tall building the ground-floor units may be less attractive because they are easier to break into.

All the above features may cause a unit to be priced below a similar "safe" unit. However, this is a case where it doesn't pay to be penny wise and pound foolish. Whenever safety is a concern, avoid purchasing the unit. It will be less desirable and more difficult to resell later on.

TIP

Look for developments with a gate or guarded entrance. People will pay more for these units (generally at least 5 percent more than for units in a competing ungated or unguarded development), and they are usually easier to resell.

Does the Unit Have an Attractive Exterior?

Just as the overall development has (or lacks) curb appeal, so do individual units. When you come up to one unit you may be greeted by a garden setting with an attractive walkway leading to the front door. The front appearance may be quite appealing. For another unit, the front door may simply be set into a blank wall. From the outside, the unit could look bleak and barren, not at all attractive.

Within any development there may be a variety of different "approaches." When you have a choice, go for the units that have attractive fronts. Avoid those with fronts that are likely to scare off potential buyers when you want to resell.

Avoid units that have the following types of entrances:

- The front door is simply set into the wall, much like a unit in an inexpensive motel.

- A party entrance leads to several units.

- There are heavy bars on the entrance doors. (Don't think you can simply remove the bars when you buy. The homeowners association may require the bars to be kept there.)

- The main entrance is from the garage or carport.

- You have to walk around several other units in order to get to your front door.

An attractive approach is as important to a shared ownership unit as good "curb appeal" is to a single-family house. It makes the unit more desirable to more people. You'll like living in it more. And you'll find it easier to resell later on.

The Design of the Unit Itself

Finally, beyond the elements of location, there's the interior of the unit you are considering. It's important to understand that when units are placed so close together, as is the case with shared ownership developments, many compromises of layout have to be made. Sometimes this results in awkward and unattractive interiors. How the unit looks on the inside is next in importance to its location.

Does It Have a Nice Layout?

Layout refers to how the rooms flow into one another. This is a tricky thing. Remember, developers must create a workable design that includes a kitchen, an eating area, several bathrooms and bedrooms, a living room, and possibly a family room all within a limited number of square feet. Layout is difficult enough when you have a house with four exterior walls to work with. However, when you have a shared ownership development with only one or at most two exterior walls for windows and light, layout can be next to impossible.

Have you ever walked into a condo, townhouse, or co-op and immediately been struck with how long and narrow the unit was? Or with how dark it seemed inside? These factors are most likely caused by the necessity of having adjacent units share wall space.

Remember, with a condo and co-op there's the possibility of other units being on both sides of yours as well as on top and below. With a townhouse there often are units on both sides. Thus, in any shared ownership dwelling, you usually give up to neighbors at least two walls that might have been used for windows. As a result, units often appear long and narrow and have poor lighting (because all the windows are typically at the front and rear).

However, well-designed units will overcome these inherent limitations. Through clever use of skylights, interior lighting, and reduced hallways, many architects have come up with shared unit layouts that appear light, spacious, and easy-flowing.

How do you know if your unit was well or poorly designed? It just takes a glance and a quick walk-through to tell. Here's what to look for:

- Lots of light flows in from windows, skylights, or even built-in artificial light sources.

- Rooms are located logically. The kitchen is next to the eating area and family room, bathrooms are away from eating areas and near bedrooms, and the living room is adjacent to the dining room or family room.

- Awkward design features—such as a staircase right behind the front door or long, dark, and narrow hallways—are kept to a minimum.

- There are few step-ups or step-downs. Some units have you going up or down to get to every room, a definite negative.

Of course, layout and design are personal matters. You may fall in love with a place I hate and vice versa. Just keep in mind, however, that you want to play the odds at resale time. You want a layout and design that most buyers will find attractive. (If you're not sure, ask a competent real estate agent to point out pluses and minuses in the design.)

Is It Big Enough?

Condos, townhouses, and co-ops come in all sizes. However, you want a unit that is both big enough for you to enjoy as well as large enough to command a reasonable price and quick resale later on. Just how large is that?

Generally speaking, the following footages apply:

- For low- to modest-priced units, minimum space usually means 1000 to 1500 square feet.

- For moderate-priced units, that's 1500 to 2200 square feet.

- For high-priced units, that's anything above 2200 square feet.

Please keep in mind that these are "rule of thumb" numbers. An 800-square-foot co-op in the heart of Manhattan may be extremely high-priced. On the other hand, a 2500-square-foot townhouse in the plains of Kansas may be very modestly priced.

Another approach is to measure how much room it takes to live comfortably. While everyone's standards differ, generally speaking a couple can feel roomy in a minimum of 1200 square feet divided up into no more than two bedrooms. Tack on 250 to 500 square feet for each additional person. (Add bedrooms, as well.)

Is It Modern?

Sometimes the older developments are the most pleasing to look at, have the best close-in locations, and, unfortunately, command the highest prices. But are they the best buys? Will they see their values stagnate in the future?

A lot depends on the amenities inside the unit, such as fixtures, appliances, and decor. As a unit ages, it becomes increasingly obsolete. And obsolescence is one reason for price declines.

When you're buying, you should be on the lookout for the following:

- Appliances are old-fashioned (no self-starters on the gas stove, for example) or just plain old.

- Fixtures are reminiscent of a particular era, say the 1950s or even the 1970s.

- Wood paneling, normally a real plus, is too dark or too light for current tastes.

- Countertops are cracked or old-fashioned. (The current rage is not for tile or laminate but for Corean® or granite.)

- Flooring or carpeting is worn, old-fashioned (for example, shag instead of plush pile), or an undesirable color.

- Cabinets need replacing, sinks are chipped or stained, and doors are hollow-core and made from inexpensive-looking materials.

Of course, all the above features can be updated and modernized. But that takes money, lots of it. A complete kitchen update, even in a condo, townhouse, or co-op, can cost $10,000 to $25,000 or more. Add another $5000 per bath, $10,000 for wood paneling and carpeting, and so on. Very quickly you can find that updating means having to spend far more than the value of the unit (the cost of modernizing plus the cost of purchase). All of which is to say that sometimes buying a newer unit, even if it apparently costs more, is actually cheaper in the long run.

TRAP

Beware of obsolescence in design. In some older units the garage enters onto the living room. In well-designed modern units it's usually onto the kitchen, to facilitate transport of groceries.

The Bottom Line

When you buy, look with your eyes, not your heart. Try to see both the pluses and the minuses to each development and unit. And always keep in mind that no matter what your current plans happen to be, chances are that a few years down the road you may want to sell. Buy a unit that will allow you to resell with ease.

3

Understanding the Rules

In the United States we pride ourselves on living by the rule of law. In fact, we are quite comfortable with having written laws in effect that govern virtually every aspect of our lives, from driving a car to smoking in public.

When we buy into a shared ownership development, we are actually acquiring additional "laws" or rules by which we must live. It's very important to understand that all shared living developments are more restrictive than developments of single-family homes. A shared ownership arrangement can positively or adversely affect our enjoyment of our unit.

TRAP

The biggest single mistake that buyers of condos, townhouses, and co-ops make is to overlook or discount the rules of the development. When you buy into a shared ownership arrangement, part of the baggage that you get is all the rules.

TIP

Shared ownership developments aren't the only housing arrangements with homeowners associations and rules. Today many single-family homes, particularly in newer developments, have an association to which owners must belong. This association primarily guards the appearance of the individual homes, striving to ensure a degree of conformity as conceived and set up by the developer. Sometimes the association oversees common areas as well.

Why More Rules?

This is probably the first question that most buyers ask when considering a shared ownership unit. Indeed, many people refuse to buy into such developments just because of the restrictive rules. I've known people who specifically avoid condos, townhouses, or co-ops because of the restrictions in their lifestyle that these impose. I've heard comments such as "I don't want anybody telling me I can't have a pet" and "Nobody's going to show me what kind of mailbox I can install."

TIP

The organization that runs a condo or townhouse development is usually called the homeowners association, or HOA (but may sometimes be called the property owners association, or POA). The organization that runs a co-op is the corporation. In both cases the governing body is the board of directors, or board, elected by the homeowners. Committees function under the guidance and approval of the board.

The simple fact is that if you don't want increased restrictions, albeit small ones, in your life, don't buy into a shared ownership development. On the other hand, there are very good reasons that you might want to abide by such rules.

There Is Conformity

The development will remain as it was originally built (or converted). And individual units usually will not be much differentiated. In other words, one unit won't stand out because it's so fixed up and another won't be prominent because it's so run down. The rules will require that *all* the units maintain a similar, equal, conforming appearance. In a well-run development, the appearance will be quite nice and the conformity of it will be a real plus when it comes time to resell, all because of the rules.

There Is Stability

When you buy a single-family home, a big consideration is your neighbors. For example, if you don't have kids in your household, you may want a quiet neighborhood with few children. On the other hand, if you've got kids, you may want a neighborhood that's got lots of playmates for them. When you buy, your neighbors may seem perfect. But neighbors sell their homes and new ones move in. How do you know your neighborhood will remain the same?

In a shared ownership development there may be rules regarding the number of children allowed per unit. There may be rules on age (for example, only those over 55 may purchase). And there will be a board or association to make sure that the character of the "neighborhood" remains the same over time. In other words, you get stability.

You Get Security

The rules may require that a fence or wall completely encircle the shared ownership development. There may be a gate and even a guard on duty to restrict those who come in.

Many developments pay for a private police force (either on site or on call from outside). If there's a problem, you can call a number and get help, usually faster than in nonshared ownership developments. In addition, there's usually someone around who can watch your place when you're gone. You can alert security that you'll be away, or you can tell neighbors who are literally right next door.

You Get Investment Potential

The restrictions and rules, as we've seen, can be a real plus, providing stability and security that encourage others to want to live in the same development as you. Over time, you can expect your property to increase in value, giving you investment potential.

Where Are the Rules Written?

The rules by which shared ownership developments [also called common interest developments (CID)] function come from two basic sources. The first are the CC&Rs (covenants, conditions, and restrictions) written into the deed to the property. The second are the bylaws and rules adopted by the owners. (For co-ops many of the rules are specified in the proprietary lease agreement between the corporation and the "tenant" owner.)

You should get a copy of the CC&Rs, bylaws, and rules adopted by the board (and the lease agreement of a co-op) before you buy. (*Note:* A board can change or adopt rules, but normally only the homeowners can change, amend, or adopt bylaws and CC&Rs.) These can usually be obtained quite easily by contacting someone on the board of directors. (The CC&Rs are recorded; hence you can always get a copy of them from a title insurance company.)

TRAP

Sometimes, for whatever reason, the management of a shared ownership development can't provide you with copies of the documents you need or refuses to do so. Either way, this is a definite "no-no" when it comes to buying. Without seeing the documents, you won't know what the rules are and you can't know what you're getting yourself into.

TIP

Many states now require that boards provide the documents to prospective buyers in a timely fashion, although they may charge a nominal fee for the service. Check with a good agent to help you here.

Once you get a copy of the documents, spend some time reading them over. They will usually be quite readable, despite occasional legalese. You may want to have your lawyer clarify certain points. But most often, you'll be able to understand them fairly easily. For example, it isn't hard to grasp the meaning of "No dogs allowed on the premises at any time."

What Are CC&Rs?

The conditions, covenants, and restrictions are the rules that govern the use of property. Usually, but not always, they are added to a property by the developer at the time the shared ownership development is built.

CC&Rs are found on virtually all real estate. Sometimes they date back to the colonial or Spanish land grant period. The CC&Rs restrict usage. For example, they may say that only a condominium development may be built. Or that no unit may be constructed smaller than 1000 square feet.

The CC&Rs "run" with the land—in other words, with the property. When you buy a condo, you get full ownership of your property and an apportioned ownership in the common area. The CC&Rs cover both. Perhaps the most important functions of the CC&Rs in a condo development are to detail the use of the common area, provide for a board of directors, and authorize the passage and use of bylaws.

In a co-op the property is essentially bought by a corporation, which then passes bylaws and rules. All new laws, however, must comply with the CC&Rs that run with the property.

TIP

It's important to understand that the rules of one shared ownership development may be significantly different from those of another. Don't make the mistake of thinking that when you've read one set of rules, you've seen them all. Each development is different, and you must receive and examine its rules to know what you're getting.

TRAP

Some CC&Rs on older properties are not enforceable. For example, there may be restrictions on the purchase of the property by people of different races or religions. Such restrictions, though still written in, have been superseded by federal and state laws that make them, in effect, null and void. Generally speaking, don't waste your time worrying about antiquated CC&Rs. They are from a different era and usually remain in the deed simply because it's technically very hard to get them removed.

Can CC&Rs Be Changed?

Yes. And no. It's a question of practicality. The CC&Rs run with the deeds of all the owners of a development. If all the owners (100 percent) get together, they can vote to change the CC&Rs.

However, when was the last time that you saw a group of people who were 100 percent agreed on anything? Hence, as a practical matter, it is difficult to change the CC&Rs.

In most modern shared ownership developments, the CC&Rs have been carefully prepared by a legal team. However, in older developments (usually 40 years or more), the CC&Rs may have been put together ad hoc by the developer. Hence, these older documents may not contain the supporting language that you'd like.

For example, in one development I visited, the CC&Rs were put together in the late 1940s by the developer. They were only one page long. (Modern CC&Rs are usually dozens, sometimes hundreds of pages long.) While the developer's short CC&Rs did call for the formation of a board of directors with the power to pass bylaws, it didn't contain language providing for architectural restrictions (which most members want) or for the increase of dues.

In the short run, the board managed to survive by passing rules to handle these matters. However, when several members challenged a dues hike needed to cover increased costs—a power that was not specifically given to the board—the directors had to back down.

Relief was ultimately provided by the state (in this case, California), which passed a statute allowing older shared ownership developments to enact changes in their CC&Rs with less than a 100 percent vote but with a supermajority. Such statutes may themselves be challenged, but where they are upheld, it becomes possible for an older development to pass new and more comprehensive CC&Rs for the benefit of its members, despite a few dissenting votes. (Under such statutes the required majority may vary but is typically from two-thirds to 90 percent.)

What Do the Bylaws Cover?

While such things as architectural requirements, rules about pets, and changes to units are usually covered in the CC&Rs, the bylaws often address how to run the association. They cover such things as how and when meetings are held and how voting should be conducted. In a well-designed development, most conceivable (and in some cases inconceivable!) circumstances are covered. That's they reason you need to make yourself familiar with the bylaws.

Can the Bylaws Be Changed?

Yes. The board of directors may frame and put together changes to the bylaws, but it usually takes a vote of the membership to adopt these changes. For example, some developments require a simple majority vote of the membership on changes to the bylaws. In the case of serious issues, such as a raise in dues, a two-thirds majority may be required. *Note:* Boards may adopt new rules (which are applications of the bylaws) without a membership vote.

TIP

In recent years, because of the unwillingness of a small group of members to allow a dues increase (in some cases, only a little over a third can block such an increase), states have passed laws allowing boards to increase dues by a maximum amount each year, regardless of what the members vote. For example, the board may be allowed to increase the dues 20 percent on its own. Again, check with a good shared ownership attorney or agent to understand the mechanism for changing bylaws in your development.

TRAP

Be alert to how votes are apportioned among members of a shared ownership development. Voting rights may be apportioned on the basis of one vote per owner. However, voting can also be apportioned according to the amount of square footage, the number of bedrooms, the location in the development, or any of a large number of other factors. You may have only one vote, but your neighbor could have two—or three!

Can the Rules Restrict Who Buys Into the Development?

Yes, they can. As noted earlier, the CC&Rs on older properties may discriminate according to race or religion. While such restrictions are now outlawed, it is still possible to discriminate by family size, age, or financial condition.

For example, a condo may have an age restriction—say, at least one family member must be 55 years old. The board may enforce this restriction and require you to provide evidence of age when you buy.

Or, a co-op board may require would-be buyers to appear before a membership committee and explain whether they are financially qualified to live there. The would-be owners may need to demonstrate that they have minimum income and financial resources. For example, you may need to bring in your last tax statements, submit a pay stub, or show proof of bank deposits. (More on this in Chapter 9.)

TIP

In a co-op the need for allowing only people of sound financial background into the property is real. There is usually a hefty mortgage on the property, and all owners are required to pay their share. If a new owner can't make the payments, then his or her share must be made up by all the other owners. To reduce the danger of default, the board or membership committee can reasonably demand to know that any would-be buyers are financially sound.

Of course, in a condo development, no such membership committee exists (except, perhaps, as a social organization). Here, the mortgage is only on your own unit and you alone are responsible for repaying it. If you don't repay, the mortgage company comes after you, not the other owners. Any mortgage on the common areas would be paid back out of dues or an assessment. (More about ownership of condos and townhouses in Chapters 7 and 8.)

Living by the Rules

The long and the short of it is that in any shared ownership development there will be lots of rules. They will both restrict and protect you. They may be the reason that some people refuse to buy in. They may also be the very reason that others want to buy in.

It's important to understand that you'll have to live by the rules. You may not agree with all of them and may want to change one or two—indeed, you may even succeed in overturning a rule here and there. For the most part, however, you'll have to live by the rules of the place when you buy.

That's why, when considering any shared ownership development, you must make it a point to get a copy of the bylaws, the Rules, and the CC&Rs (and the lease in a co-op) and read all the documents carefully. You don't want any unpleasant surprises later on.

4

Seven "Red Flag" Questions You Must Ask Before You Buy

If you're considering the purchase of a condo, townhouse, or co-op, you're getting involved in a big investment. Today prices are typically well over $100,000. In some areas they can be far, far higher.

In addition, because of the nature of shared ownership, you're jumping on board a ship with a bunch of other people and once that ship sails, you'll be taken wherever it goes. If it's in poor financial condition and sinks, you could go down with it. In some cases, you could even be liable for losses in addition to what you've invested in your property!

This warning is not intended to scare you away from a condo, townhouse, or co-op. It's merely to advise you that buying is serious business. No matter how wonderful the property seems at first glance, you need to go deeper and to ask important questions that will help you discover its true financial condition. Those are the questions we'll ask in this chapter.

1. What Is the Tenant-to-Owner Ratio?

The ratio of tenants to owners can seriously affect the quality of lifestyle as well as the financial future in a development. Tenants rent dwelling units from owners. Put most simply, the more tenants and fewer owners who reside at the property, the less attractive it is.

Much of the reason has to do with pride of ownership, an important factor in all real estate. It's an established fact that owners take better care of their property than do tenants. They are more observant of rules, they tend to keep the place in better shape, and they are more considerate of their neighbors.

This is not to say that all tenants are terrible. It's just that tenants don't have the huge financial stake in the property they occupy that owners do. If things don't work out, they can move out in a month and find another rental. If you're an owner, it's not so easy.

If a development has a lot of tenants, you're likely to find that overall it's a noisier place. Generally the swimming pool, spa, and other amenities may be more heavily used, there are more problems with maintaining the common areas, and so on. On the other hand, if the development is almost entirely owner-occupied, you'll tend to find it quieter and cleaner, with less demand on the amenities.

There's another, more ominous reason for checking the tenant-to-owner ratio. If a development is difficult to resell or there are problems with living there, often the owners will move out and will rent their units to help offset their mortgage and other costs. In other words, they can't stand living there themselves and they can't resell, so they rent out. This is the worst type of situation, one into which you would be well advised not to buy.

What are the ratios to watch out for? Any development with a ratio of 10 percent tenants or less should be considered good; 20 percent or more tenants should be considered a serious detracting feature. Anything in between 10 and 20 percent is a gray area that could be good or bad depending on how the other questions (below) are answered.

TIP

Some mortgage lenders won't offer loans on shared ownership properties when the ratio is 25 to 30 percent tenants or higher! You may have trouble getting financing to buy in and then, later on, have trouble reselling because future buyers face similar financing problems.

2. Are There Any Lawsuits Pending?

Lawsuits are the bane of shared ownership developments. They can pull down an association and drive the owners to financial ruin.

The lawsuits can be from outside, as when an employee sues the association for wrongful termination or when a guest slips and falls and is injured. Suits can also be from within, as when one owner sues the association over a grievance, such as not allowing a certain type of vehicle to be parked or refusing to allow alterations within the unit. (Most owner suits come about when the association attempts to uphold the rules and regulations of the development.)

Or the suit could be brought by the homeowners association, for example, against the builder/developer for shoddy work (as when the roofs leak) or against an individual owner for failure to pay dues on time.

The big problem with lawsuits is liability. If the association (or the board) loses, the homeowners (who are the association) lose. That means that a judgment could be awarded against all the owners and each one could be required to pay a portion of it. (Some states limit such loss, provided there is sufficient liability insurance.)

Be sure you're clear on what this means. If there's a lawsuit pending when you buy into a condo, townhouse, or co-op and the association or governing board subsequently loses the suit and must pay damages, you could be liable for your share of those damages. If the damages are high, in the millions of dollars, you could be liable for payment of thousands or tens of thousands of dollars, depending on how many owners the damages are spread over. This could occur even if you bought in after the lawsuit was filed.

It is for this reason that you want to know *if* there are any pending lawsuits. If so, get all possible information on them and then have a competent attorney advise you of your risk. In some cases, there will be little to no risk at all because of insurance coverage. In others, the risk may be heavy.

Further, you want to know what the history of lawsuits has been for the development. Even though no suits may be pending at the moment, if over the last 10 years there have been several, you may want to reconsider your purchase. The development, for whatever reason, may be a fractious place where lawsuits occur all the time. Perhaps this is simply a quiet period between suits; they could crop up again after you buy.

(See also the next question, with regard to insurance.)

TRAP

Lenders may be just as acutely concerned about lawsuits are you are. Sometimes buyers cannot get good financing if lawsuits are pending. The good lenders are simply scared away. That means that not only will you have trouble financing your purchase, but you could have trouble reselling later on as potential buyers encounter similar financing difficulties.

3. How Much Insurance Does the Board Carry?

There are two concerns here: liability and disasters.

The answer to lawsuits can be insurance. If the development carries enough liability insurance, the owners can be covered in the event there's a lawsuit and damages are awarded against them.

Then there's the matter of disasters—hurricanes, earthquakes, floods, land slippage, and so on. These call for special insurance, and typically the individual owner cannot buy it. It's available only if the entire development buys it through the homeowners association or the board of directors.

However, insurance can be tricky. You need to know how much insurance the development carries (is it enough?) and what it covers. Also, what are the deductibles the homeowner is responsible for? These can be very high.

How Much Liability Insurance?

In terms of liability, my own feeling is that any development I belong to should have at least $3 million in liability coverage. If the development includes common areas and amenities, particularly pools or spas, the figure goes up very quickly. I would not consider $10 or $15 million excessive in a large development.

The liability coverage should include damages awarded as the result of a lawsuit from any cause. Unfortunately, that's not always possible. Insurance companies may be unwilling to cover areas of real risk. You should be particularly concerned that the development has liability coverage on:

- Accidents (as when someone slips and falls on the concrete next to a pool or spa)

- Actions of the board—errors and omissions (as when the board acts against an owner and that owner in retaliation sues and wins)

- Actions of employees (as when someone is hurt through negligence of the board or is wrongfully terminated)

- Actions of owners (as when someone doesn't like a rule and goes to court to get it changed)

TIP

If the development never has any lawsuits, chances are it can get excellent, high-level coverage for a minimal cost. In other words, the maxim applies: If you don't need insurance, you can easily get it. If, however, there have been many lawsuits (even if the development has always won), insurers may be reluctant to offer complete coverage or high levels of coverage; or they may charge premiums so high that getting the insurance becomes impractical.

How Much Disaster Insurance?

The problem here is that while you can get excellent hurricane coverage in California, which almost never has hurricanes, you can't get very good earthquake insurance, yet earthquakes are a real threat. The opposite is true in Florida.

It's a real plus if a development has insurance to cover likely disasters. It means that if you buy, your purchase will be more secure and you may even find it easier to get financing. However, the result will almost always be significantly higher monthly assessments (dues).

TRAP

You usually can't get insurance on your own to cover earthquakes, floods, hurricanes, and other disasters. If coverage is available at all, it's usually available only if the entire development takes it out. Check it out.

Find out what disaster insurance the development you're considering has, then ask a competent insurance agent to evaluate the coverage. If there's a problem with insurance, you want to know about it up front. If the risk is severe, you may want to back out of your purchase.

4. Are the Reserves Adequate?

Everything wears out over time. In a shared ownership development, that includes items outside your individual unit. (Inside things wear out, too, but they're your responsibility.) We're talking here about the roof, paint on the exterior walls, a clubhouse, a swimming pool pump and heater, walkways (which crack and need to be fixed or replaced), a foundation (which can sag or break), and so on. The question becomes: Where does the money come from to fix these items?

A well-run development will have reserve funds set aside to cover all the things that wear out—to cover future major repairs and replacements. For example, there will be a roof replacement reserve. Perhaps only $2000 a year is added to this account. However, over 25 years it will amount to $50,000 plus interest, probably enough to cover the cost of replacing the roof.

Perhaps only $250 a year is placed in the pool reserve. But after 10 years, there's $2500 plus interest to cover a new pump and filter. And so on.

TIP

Be careful if you are buying into a development that has a lot of amenities, such as a golf course, tennis court, clubhouse, swimming pool, and spa. These all require expensive maintenance: the tennis court needs resurfacing, the golf course needs new mowers and a new watering system, the pool needs replastering, and so on. Check to see if the maintenance work has already been done or if it remains to be done. Needed repairs could be costly. And if no reserves are in place to handle the costs, you could be looking at special assessments and big regular assessment increases in the near future.

TRAP

Beware of a development that structures its reserves on overly short or long expected life periods for equipment. Some things wear out in 5 or 10 years. Others, such as buildings, may take 30 to 50 years or more to wear out. A good development will build into its reserves a realistic lifespan for each type of property.

Ideally in a shared ownership arrangement, reserves are set up to cover all the things that wear out. Each year money from assessments is set aside and when something does break or wear out, the money is there to cover it.

Unfortunately, this is the exception rather than the rule. In most cases, the owners are concerned with the short term—that is, keeping their dues low. Thus, instead of collecting enough money each month and each year for reserves, the development collects only enough for current operating costs. As a result, when something wears out and needs to be replaced, there's no money available to cover it.

Where does the money come from, then? If there are no ready reserves, the association or board will usually borrow the money and then assess each owner for the cost. As a result, the regular assessments could suddenly jump up to pay for the loan.

Generally speaking, owners can get away with not funding reserves during the early years of a development's life. Usually during the first 20 years, big-ticket items such as reroofing, complete repainting, and new heating or cooling systems are not needed. Thus, everyone gets by with low dues payments and there's little penalty.

However, it is during those early years that reserve money should be accumulating to cover items that are going to wear out just over the horizon. If you're buying into a development when it's brand new, check to see if reserves have been set up and are being funded. (See Chapter 5 for a typical reserve account statement.)

If you're buying into an older development, check to see that sizable reserves are already in place to cover the above items. If there are no reserves, chances are you could be in for a rude awakening one morning when your assessment skyrockets.

TIP

In some older developments the reserves will be low, not because enough money wasn't set aside, but because a major problem has just been fixed. For example, the reserve for painting could be near zero because the building was just repainted. There is nothing wrong with this as long as there's a plan to refund the reserve for the next painting.

TRAP

Some states now require associations to set up and fund reserves. Be sure to check with an agent or attorney to see if your state has such a requirement and if the development you are planning to buy into is in compliance. (If it's not in compliance, not only will it eventually need to raise dues to make repairs, but it may be subject to state penalties as well!)

5. Have There Been Big Hikes in Assessments?

Have there been frequent *big* assessment hikes? The board should be able to provide you with a history. It should show you what each member has paid in assessments since the development opened.

In addition to adequate reserves, noted above, you should look for a long history of stable assessments. This does not mean that costs haven't increased. Inflation requires that they increase just to maintain the same level of service. Just make sure that there haven't been any big bumps along the way to suggest that unpleasant surprises have occurred.

TRAP

Be wary of a development in which lots of owners are withholding payment of their regular assessments as a protest and the board is considering taking legal action to enforce payment. This suggests an ongoing conflict that may result in lawsuits and, potentially, special assessments to pay for legal fees and even damages. It's a bad sign and means you should reconsider your purchase. (Of course, a few people will always be in arrears—it's large numbers of people in arrears to watch out for.)

Sudden spikes in dues may be caused by inadequate reserves to meet unexpected repairs, damage awards in a lawsuit, or even a poor job of management. The governing board may have exceeded its budget before the end of the fiscal year and may need to levy a special assessment to cover the unexpected debt. Poor management usually means extra costs for you.

If there was (or currently is) a spike or a special assessment, you need to inquire as to the reason. Find out what happened and why, and factor that information into your decision to purchase.

TRAP

Check out the recent annual financial report of the board or association. If you're not sure how to read it, take it to your accountant. The report can let you know whether the development is well run and meeting its budget or is in debt and a financial mess.

Special assessments may be a onetime or rare occurrence that you need not worry about. However, if there are many spikes, it could indicate a recurring pattern of serious problems.

TIP

You can often find out the real reason behind a large special assessment just by talking with the general manager or members of the board of directors. If they are not helpful, find out who was on the board at the time of the spike (the information should be readily available) and call the old board members. Often, they will gladly inform you of what the situation was.

6. Are You Responsible for Any Areas Other Than Inside Your Unit?

As the owner of a condo, townhouse, or co-op, you are responsible for the maintenance of the inside of your unit. But are there any other areas of responsibility?

Not long ago, while considering the purchase of a townhouse, I noticed that the association did not have a reserve for roof replacement. Since it had other reserves, I asked why there was none for the roof.

I was told that each individual owner (me if I bought in) was responsible for his or her own roof! Since the development was nearly 25 years old, I immediately checked it out. In some cases the roofs were new, having recently been replaced by owners. In other cases they were older and obviously worn. In the townhouse

I was considering, the roof had recently been replaced, so I wasn't overly concerned. However, if the roof had been worn, it would have been a costly expense for me (or the next owner) to bear individually.

Other areas of individual owner responsibility may include landscaping immediately outside the unit, painting outside walls and windows of the unit, and other items. In one case I discovered a condo where the owners adjacent to the driveways leading out of the development were responsible for logo signs!

Don't assume that everything outside the unit you are considering is handled by the development. You might wake up one morning to find that you and you alone have an expensive item to fix.

7. Are There Any Rules You Can't Live With?

This is a very big consideration. Shared ownership developments live and die by their rules. As an owner, you should want strict rules, since they protect you from your neighbors and ensure a stable appearance and lifestyle. However, sometimes there are rules that you simply can't abide.

For example, it may be a seniors-only development (people only 55 and over may buy in) with a regulation that prohibits children from using the swimming pool. Yet you plan on having your grandchildren over. Will you want to keep them out of the pool? Or will that be a hardship for you?

TIP

It's a good idea to attend at least one homeowner's meeting *before* you purchase. You'll get a sense of who else is living there and, judging from how the meeting is run, whether the development is managed well and the rules are strictly enforced.

Or you have a motor home (or motorcycle) and plan to park it adjacent to your unit. Yet the rules prohibit parking such vehicles overnight.

Or you love the unit, but it's a bit too small and you plan to enlarge by adding a bedroom off the back, where there's plenty of room. But the rules prohibit making changes of any kind without specific board approval.

Or your unit is near the lake, which is the central feature of the development, but a dirt road comes down right next to your house, allowing lake access to others. After you buy, you plan to close the road. Only the dirt road is a deeded access route for the other homeowners and you won't be able to close it.

Or...you get the picture. You love the development, but there are one or two rules that you just can't abide.

If that's the case, don't purchase. The chances of you being able to change the rules once you're an owner are minimal. Often it takes approval by the board of directors. Sometimes, it takes approval of the other owners, *all* the other owners!

TRAP

You need to read the rules, bylaws, and CC&Rs carefully before you buy. Don't be stopped if someone from the board doesn't readily offer you the bylaws. You're entitled to see them. Sometimes you will be charged a fee for the paperwork—pay it; you need to know. Don't buy unless and until you have a copy of the bylaws and have had time to read it.

I've been on boards of shared ownership developments and I can tell you that the most disappointed owners are those who bought with high hopes of changing "just a little stupid rule." Only later did they find out that for whatever reason, other homeowners were opposed to the change. Remember, often only one or two adamant opponents can prevent the change.

Be comfortable with all the rules before you buy. Otherwise, stay away.

I consider these seven questions the most important ones to ask before you buy into a shared ownership development. Of course, there are many other questions and items that you need to know, and we'll discuss them in the following chapters. But if you've got these answered, you're a long way toward making an informed and intelligent purchase decision.

5

Checking Out the Board

If you've never been to a board of directors meeting for a condo, townhouse, or co-op development, you've missed out on one of life's more entertaining moments. Indeed, you owe it to yourself to attend at least one meeting before buying a unit in the development. After all, these are the people who will be setting the rules and governing a significant portion of your life after you make your purchase.

To set the record straight, the governing body for shared ownership developments is the board of directors. The board acts as a judiciary, interpreting the bylaws by which the organization is guided. It acts as a legislature, determining and then adopting new rules and ordinances as needed. And it usually hires and supervises a manager who acts as an executive, making day-to-day operating decisions.

Technically the board is nothing more than the governing body of a corporation. But in effect, it's like all the branches of government rolled into one. In other words, the board has lots of power within the shared ownership development.

Why People Run for the Board

This power is the reason that many owners run for the board. I belong to several shared ownership developments and I find that when it comes time to elect new board members, the campaigning is equal to that of a general public election.

I've seen hopeful board candidates literally spend thousands of dollars on flyers, advertisements, even "gifts" to owners in the hopes of winning their votes. All this to gain election to a board that typically pays no salary, offers no fringe benefits, requires untold hours of time and work, and leads to no higher political office.

TRAP

 The converse is sometimes true. I've seen associations where no one wanted to run for the board and it was like pulling teeth trying to get "volunteers." Usually this is the case when there is very little common property and things are running so well that no one feels the need to help out, a real rarity!

Some board members have a specific agenda. They may want to get new equipment for the golf course or new concrete for the tennis court or covered parking for guest spaces. Their specific reasons are endless, but they believe their only recourse is to run for the board and gain power to accomplish their agenda.

Other board members simply crave power for itself. They long to be in a position to impose their will on others. You can easily identify them. The power seekers speak at length at board meetings, even over extremely minor points, being sure their point of view is heard. Then they cast their votes in as dramatic a way as possible.

Finally, there are the new owners, perhaps people such as you. You may, indeed, have your own agenda—some rule you'd like added, reversed, or amended—and may feel compelled to run for the board to accomplish your goal. Or you may, indeed, have a desire for power. But more than likely, you will run for the board in defense, to protect yourself, and others, from people in the first two categories. You will want to see that the organization runs smoothly, that the board doesn't take foolish action resulting in a lawsuit against the organization (you), and that things move along fairly and in an even-handed fashion.

You and the Board

You'll notice I said that you'll *want* to run for the board. In all likelihood this is not something you're even dreaming about when you buy. But once you've purchased, you'll find that little things begin adding up until you simply can't stand the status quo and begin to feel that the only means to right wrongs and keep the development from going astray is for you to get on the board and do something. After a year or two or three, you're suddenly a candidate for the board.

And chances are you'll win election! If your motivation is simply to do a good job, other owners will recognize that and will want to have you on the board representing them. Indeed, you may even be asked to run.

Once elected, you'll serve typically from one to three years, depending on how the board in your development is structured. You'll attend weekly, biweekly, or monthly meetings. You'll sit in on special financial and other planning sessions. You'll hear personnel matters in special closed-door meetings.

At general meetings, which are open to all owners, you may frequently find yourself in firefights. As a board member, I have often been asked to vote on matters that seriously divided the membership. For example, I can recall once having to decide whether to have an older member's driveway snowplowed in winter. The rules said no individual driveways would be plowed, but this member was old and infirm and needed extra help. Certainly, out of compassion, I would vote in the affirmative.

Yet this would set a precedent and then other members would ask to have their driveways plowed. The added expense of doing it for everyone could become significant, ultimately resulting in an assessment increase. So, from a sound financial perspective, naturally I would vote in the negative. I didn't know how to vote!

The battle raged on for meeting after meeting. Some members were for, others against. Sometimes members would get so enraged they would stand up and call me or another board member a liar or worse. Other times members of different factions would scuffle among themselves.

How did it turn out? To tell you the truth, I don't really remember which way I voted or the ultimate outcome! The point is that a little matter ballooned out of proportion and became the source of heated and sometimes prolonged debate. It's something you'll certainly face as a board member.

If you're particularly energetic, you may be elected president of the board. You'll have to attend all sorts of functions and be there when almost any decision is made. It's virtually a full-time position regardless of how big or small the development is.

And after a year or two, you'll get sick of it. You'll come to despise the other owners, who seem selfish and short-sighted. You'll dislike the other board members, who can't see things as clearly and as quickly as you and who often, in your opinion, vote wrongly. You'll resent the time "wasted" on required board functions.

Very likely if your term is for more than a year, you'll resign early in disgust and refuse to have anything more to do with the board or the organization. In some cases you may be so disillusioned by what you've been through that you'll sell your unit and move to a single-family development that has no shared ownership or board.

However, if you're determined, you'll stick out your term and retire gracefully. Thereafter you'll be called upon when the new board needs someone with your expertise. And you'll mellow, realizing the frailties of men and women and accepting them as just another part of life. You won't become bitter, but will be willing to help out here and there as you can.

If you think I've painted an overly dramatic picture of the board or wrongly estimated your desire to join, all I can say is, wait. Perhaps you'll be lucky. Maybe in your case the board won't operate like a dysfunctional family. Things will run smoothly and you'll find no need to interfere yourself. It's just that I've belonged to many shared ownership organizations, and I've seen the pattern of new owner to unsatisfied owner to board member to burned-out member too often to think it happens only in isolated cases.

How Do I Evaluate a Board of Directors?

When you're new to the association or corporation, it can be hard to evaluate how well run the board is. But there are a number of clues.

Is the Board Active, Proactive, or Passive?

Talk to a couple of board members. They should be pleased to chat with you either in person or over the phone.

TIP

If you can't get hold of board members or they refuse to talk with you, a serious problem may exist between the board and the membership. No board member should be too busy to spare a few moments for a chat with a potential new owner.

Ask if the board mainly initiates policy or waits for issues to come up from the membership. You don't want a board that goes looking for trouble. On the other hand, you don't want a board that does nothing until real damage has occurred.

Is There a Newsletter?

During my tenure on one board, there were constant hard feelings between board members and owners, mostly arising out of misunderstandings and lack of information. So I started a newsletter that published the minutes of meetings as well as articles on what the board was doing. Almost overnight the misunderstandings vanished.

TIP

If you want to start a newsletter for your development, talk to the local newspaper. It may be willing to publish the newsletter free in exchange for running advertisements that reach the members. I have done this on several occasions and it usually works out well.

How Are the Meetings Conducted?

A well-run board will have well-ordered meetings. Typically some time will be allotted for owners to speak from the floor, but most of the meeting will be devoted to board members handling deliberations over a carefully prepared agenda.

TRAP

Beware of board meetings where disorder rules. Here owners in the audience often stand up and interrupt board members, shouting out comments and sometimes epithets during the meeting. Often arguments between owners in the audience will overshadow discussion by the board. Here the meetings are out of control, little to nothing gets done, and animosities deepen. This kind of board should be replaced. Perhaps even better, you should reconsider your purchase into the development.

Does the Development Have a Web Site?

Currently it costs $70 for a domain (Web site) for two years and around $20 a month for a host to run it. Usually there's an owner who would be thrilled to set up the site, and after that minimal effort should be required to update it.

For the minimal effort, however, the Web site can offer members and others all kinds of information about the development. It can broadcast news, gather feedback on important issues (using e-mail), and generally provide community information. Increasingly homeowners associations and co-op corporations are putting up their own Web sites. It's a real plus if yours has one.

Is the Management Professional?

We'll discuss professional management in depth later. At this point, when you're considering buying, you want someone to talk to. This should be a general manager who can provide you with copies of bylaws and other documents you need.

The worst situation is when no one is running the show. You call up and get an answering machine with the promise that a board member will call back. And that person never does.

The Duties of the Board

Now that you understand the perils of belonging to the board of directors, let's get down to what the actual duties of the board are. They include:

1. Protecting, maintaining, and enhancing the assets of the community
2. Establishing an operating budget
3. Setting up reasonable reserves
4. Collecting assessments (dues)
5. Making rules for the common good
6. Dealing with requests for alterations
7. Handling the operation of the organization

How Does the Board Protect the Development and Owners?

Protection is probably the most important function of the board. Every development has restrictions intended to promote a particular look and feel. They run the gamut from seeing to it that specific colors are painted on the exterior walls, to making certain that common lawns are mowed, to restricting the size and style of "For Rent" signs owners put up. This protective role ensures that the development doesn't deteriorate as a result of improper activities or negligence.

A board that is diligent in exercising its protective duties will help ensure that the entire development maintains its value. When it comes time for you to resell, some of the very restrictions that you chafe at will be the ones that attract buyers to your unit.

Conformity, regularity, and intolerance of difference are the watchwords of well-run boards. Rules protect you from other owners.

Suppose you buy a single-family home without a homeowners association. What do you do if your neighbor paints her home purple, throws parties all hours of the night, or has dogs that bark incessantly? Often your only recourse is the police (who may be of little help). Or you might try a lawsuit, with a doubtful outcome. On the other hand, a board can enforce restrictions on painting and noise and pets, and quickly get the matter in hand.

A well-run board sees to it that the entire development maintains minimal protective standards. If you like those standards, you will want to support the board in its efforts.

Why Does the Board Need an Operating Budget?

Often the first complaint of a new member is the cost of dues. What are they going for? Why are they needed at all? Why not just do away with the budget?

I once belonged to a board that decided just that—cut the dues down to 25 percent and eliminate all the services that otherwise had to be paid for. Needless to say, most of the membership was thrilled, at first.

But what was eliminated was what everyone counted on from the development: maintenance of common areas, a manager on duty to handle problems, reserves to cover repairs and replacement of worn-out areas, and so on.

TIP

All members want lower dues. But no members want reduced services.

One of the most important functions of the board is to determine what services are required, to estimate accurately how much they will cost, and then to set up a budget to cover them. As in a household, good budgeting results in knowing what your needed expenses are and having the money on hand to pay for them.

TRAP

Beware of boards that want to cut amenities, such as closing down the swimming pool and spa, to save money and reduce dues. It's usually penny wise and pound foolish. The amenities are often what attract people to the development in the first place. You may lower assessments, temporarily, but you'll also reduce the real estate value of your unit.

When Should the Board Set Up Reasonable Reserves?

Some states require that boards establish reserves on a regular basis. California, for example, requires all boards, regardless of the size of the development, to determine the life of all assets and create reserves to replace them. Other states are more lenient.

A large part of the budget each year should be set aside in reserve. The best approach is to have an accounting firm determine the lifespan of roofs, vehicles, and other assets, then decide how much money should be set aside, including accrued interest and an accounting for inflation, for replacement.

TIP

Check out how long the reserves anticipate replacements. Sometimes the expected lifespan is given as 10 years. But buildings may not wear out for 30 to 50 years. A good reserve program will anticipate up to at least 30 years for some types of property.

TRAP

Beware of reserve funds that are cast in stone. Interest rates and inflation fluctuate, and a reserve fund should be flexible enough to take these changes into account each year.

For smaller developments, simply hiring an outside firm to set up the reserve account can be a financial burden, so an owner who is familiar with accounting procedures may take on the task. If that member is competent, the arrangement can work very well.

What's important is that the board establishes reasonable lifespans for all assets and sets up reserves to replace them. The result may be somewhat large dues initially, but in the long run huge special assessments to cover replacement will be avoided.

Here's a typical statement covering reserves:

Component	Estimated remaining useful life	Estimated future replacement cost	This year's reserve	Total in reserve
Building	50 yrs	$ 835,000	$13,916	$ 41,748
Equipment	22 yrs	65,000	2,600	7,800
Fencing	7 yrs	15,000	1,500	4,500
Flooring	10 yrs	23,000	2,000	6,000
Landscaping	20 yrs	120,000	5,000	15,000
Paint	7 yrs	30,000	3,750	11,250
Pool equipment	10 yrs	7,000	600	1,800
Rec. building	30 yrs	45,000	1,500	4,500
Roads/paths	10 yrs	240,000	22,000	66,000
Roof	25 yrs	30,000	1,100	3,300
Vehicles	6 yrs	25,000	4,000	12,000
Total		$1,435,000	$57,966	$173,898

TIP

The reason it's usually a good idea to have an accountant set up the reserve account is that the allowable lifespans for specific types of assets are established by state and federal guidelines. Further, the interest accrued by money set in reserve will, presumably, offset the total amount that needs to be collected. On the other hand, inflation, which eats into the money saved, must be accounted for as well. (If guesses regarding inflation are off, the entire schedule needs to be adjusted. Reviews should be made annually.) Getting reasonably good future estimates is an important function of setting up the reserves.

What Must the Board Do to Collect Assessments?

However we feel about the IRS, without it there would be no federal government and none of the services it performs for defense, education, and so on. Just as the government lives on tax money, the shared ownership association lives on assessments from members (plus other fees it may command from vending machines, sales of equipment, and so on).

It's up to the board to see to it that assessments are set high enough to cover the estimated annual budget and then to ruthlessly collect them. Unfortunately, dues policy can sometimes produce hard feelings among owners.

Often the not-so-hidden agenda of members who run for the board is to keep assessments low and stable, no matter what. In other cases, members may refuse to vote an increase, no matter what. As a result, a board may be hamstrung when it needs to raise assessments to meet operating costs and reserves.

As noted earlier, many states now allow boards to raise dues a certain minimum, perhaps 5 to 20 percent a year, without a direct vote of the membership. This coupled with requirements for maintaining reserves has pushed some reluctant boards and memberships into increasing dues to the point where adequate reserves and operating expenses can be maintained.

TRAP

 There's a danger when assessments go too high. Besides the fact that high dues can be hard for members to pay, they make resale very difficult. If you were offered two different condominium developments and all else was equal, would you choose to buy the one that had assessments of $125 a month or $325 a month? A good board will walk a fine line in raising dues high enough to meet reserves and operating requirements yet not so high as to lower property values.

Sometimes owners refuse or simply can't pay their assessments. Then it becomes the board's duty to handle enforcement, usually by friendly reminders and even personal phone calls.

What happens if the owner is intransigent? In the case of a co-op, the board may force sale of the unit to obtain back dues. In the case of a condo or townhouse, a lien may be placed on the property for the dues. (The owner of a condo or townhouse has fee simple title, not ownership of shares, so judicial foreclosure may be necessary.)

Why Does the Board Need to Make New Rules?

As we saw in the last chapter, the bylaws of the association or corporation as well as the CC&Rs determine what can and cannot be done within a development. Typically these rules are quite strict and comprehensive.

Nevertheless, there are always unanticipated situations that crop up, forcing the Board to take action. For example, some members want to hang flags or banners from their units. Other members object. There may be no mention of such things in the bylaws or CC&Rs, so the board has to act. Typically, the board will be empowered to make new rules in such circumstances.

Why Must the Board Handle Requests for Alterations?

Inevitably owners will want to make changes. If these changes are entirely within their units and do not involve the building structure, then generally speaking there is little the board can or will say about them.

On the other hand, if the changes are visible or affect the structure of the building, then the board will want to rule on them. The alteration may be major (an owner wants to enlarge a window or add a room) or minor (the owner wants to change the size or shape of a mailbox). Anything affecting the exterior or structure usually requires board approval.

Of course, in most cases the board will not rule without hearing from the architectural committee. Indeed this committee in some organizations is more powerful than the board itself! (We'll look at the role of the architectural committee in the next chapter.)

Sometimes the rule change will be so pervasive that the board will conduct an informal survey of the members to check out their thinking. Or the board may put the changes up for vote at the next annual meeting (where all members normally vote on major issues). In most cases, however, the board will put the rule change on its regular meeting agenda, discuss it, perhaps carry it forward a meeting or two to allow members to comment, and then vote it in or out.

What About Overall Operations?

The board must oversee overall operations. However, since most board members are volunteers who typically have time for meetings only after work in the evenings or on weekends, professional management is usually employed.

Obtaining professional management is a good idea. It means that there is always someone on duty to answer questions, whether by an existing owner or a prospective buyer. In addition, rules and regulations on shared ownership developments are put forth regularly by state and sometimes local and federal government agencies. Presumably a professional manager will be up on these new regulations and will see to it that your development is in compliance.

TIP

You don't need to have a large shared ownership organization to afford professional management. Some pro managers handle a large group of small developments and their fees are, correspondingly, smaller. Just check with other developments.

In addition to overseeing management, the board must handle the following matters.

Obtain Adequate Insurance. As noted earlier, I consider $3 million to be the minimum liability insurance for developments with no special risk factors such as pools and spas. Insurance should be obtained for individual board members as well as the corporation, in case specific members are sued for their actions. There is also the matter of obtaining disaster insurance.

Pay For and Direct Maintenance and Repairs.   Somebody has to be hired to mow the laws and paint the fences. Someone must get bids for replacing roofs. This is the job of the board.

Handle Personnel.   In larger developments there may be swimming pool guards, security people, groundskeepers, secretarial staff, and so on. The board has the ultimate responsibility for hiring and firing personnel. To avoid problems here, such as wrongful termination suits, it's helpful to have a professional manager who can do these jobs competently.

Deal With Legal Matters Such as Lawsuits and Claims.   When the development is sued, it's the board that must take up the defense. This includes hiring competent attorneys and investigators. In addition, the board may need to file lawsuits against the developer, construction workers, or even members who fail to comply with rules and regulations.

6

Beware the Architectural Committee!

Also beware the security and financial committees and even the board! In other words, watch out if you want to do things differently or get caught doing something against the rules.

When Would I Come Up Against Committees or the Board?

Anytime you want to make a change in your unit that can be seen from the outside or that affects the structure, you'll need to get permission, usually from an architectural committee. Anytime you break a rule, you'll be hauled up, usually before the security committee. Anytime you don't pay your dues promptly, usually the financial committee will want to talk to you. And anytime you protest the rulings of any of these committees, you'll have to face the board itself. In short, it's going to be fairly difficult to live in a shared ownership development and not have to face these people at one time or another.

For example, I recently put up a DSS satellite dish on a townhouse unit I own in a shared ownership development. A satellite dish allows me to receive television signals directly from space. The signal is digital, far higher in quality than what can be obtained from many local cable companies or by air from most TV stations. (This is not to be confused with high-quality HDTV signals, which are currently available, in limited form, from all three sources.) The real reason I wanted the dish up, however, was that it allowed me to receive every Sunday NFL football game of the season!

When satellite dishes first came out, many neighbors of dish owners protested that the units were unsightly. (Of course, these were the huge versions, sometimes as much as 12 feet across. Current models are only about 18 inches across.) So the federal government, pushed by the satellite broadcast industry, passed a law mandating that those who want to put up dishes, as part of the right to free speech, must be allowed to do so, as long as the dishes are reasonably located so as not to bother neighbors.

It's that last sentence that's the catch. The development can determine *where* the dish can be placed. So I called the board and was told by the general manager, who worked for an independent management firm, to stick it on the roof. I did.

However, as such it was visible to a neighbor, who complained bitterly that the dish looked "ugly." The neighbor demanded I take it down and, when I refused, wrote a formal complaint to the board. Shortly thereafter I received a letter from the architectural committee noting that I had not properly secured architectural approval for the dish and demanding that I relocate it.

One day the following week I was visited by the architectural committee, which informed me that regardless of what the general manager had said, I had to remove the dish from the roof and place it along a back fence, near the ground, where it couldn't be seen by anyone but me—and where, incidentally, it could barely receive an adequate signal. My choice was to comply or fight the committee.

TIP

A board can't refuse permission for you to put up a satellite dish—by federal law you're allowed to have one. However, it can regulate the appearance and location, as long as you can still receive a signal.

I meekly complied and the matter was settled.

You, too, may come up against the architectural or some other committee. All it takes is for you to want to make a change, or to break a rule. For the remainder of this chapter we'll look into how you can successfully survive such an encounter with your skin intact.

By the way, the reason I complied meekly was that it was the graceful and least expensive way out (in terms of time, money, and blood pressure). The change of location was easily accomplished, I could still see the ball games, and I didn't have to engage in a protracted and bitter fight. Compromise is still the best solution in these matters.

How Do I Handle Myself When Seeking to Make a Change?

The best policy is to attempt to work with the powers that be. That means ask permission *before* you do anything, even if you think permission isn't required. And then, if you can't get permission, seek to work out a compromise.

TIP

Always keep in mind that those who belong to the architectural committee or the board are your neighbors. You have to live with and next to them. Picking a fight is a no-win situation.

My experience is that most architectural committee members really have the good of the shared ownership community in mind. They know what the rules are and they seek to ensure that any changes conform to regulations. They're just trying to maintain the standards of the development.

Seeking their permission is obvious if you want to do something major, such as knock out a window and add a deck. Sometimes, however, the changes you want to make may appear trivial, so small that asking permission seems silly. For example, you may want to put a coat of varnish on your front door, or change your mailbox, or add your name over your doorway, or change the shrubbery in front of your unit. Yet doing any of these things could change the appearance of your unit, and the bylaws probably prohibit such changes.

The best way to avoid problems is always to ask permission first. You'll quickly be told if you can make the change you want. If not, you can try to work out a compromise. This is usually far better than forging ahead and then being faced with having to undo what you've done, with your ego fully involved.

TRAP

 If you don't like the imposition of strict rules on what you can and can't change, then you may be better off not buying into a shared ownership development. Remember, the rules are there to protect *all* owners, including you. They keep your neighbor from painting her unit purple or from putting in a mailbox in the shape of a fish. The rules that may annoy you also protect you. They ensure that the whole development will maintain certain architectural standards.

How Do I Handle Myself When I Have Been Fined for Breaking a Rule?

Making amends can be very frustrating. Typically you're angry at yourself for breaking the rule. Then you're doubly angry at the development for recognizing you did something wrong and triply angry that you received a fine. Nevertheless, a cool head can help.

I belong to a development that owns its own roads and has strict speed limits. It even has a small security force that hands out tickets to those who speed. Often those who receive tickets get quite angry and, instead of paying the fine, choose to appear before the security committee to protest.

The situation is not unlike appearing before a judge. If the accused (you or me or whoever broke the rule) appears calm and presents extenuating circumstances for what happened, often things get settled amicably. If it's a first offense, the fine may be eliminated and a warning issued instead. If it's a second offense, the fine may be reduced.

On the other hand, if the accused rants and raves about unfairness, challenges the committee's authority, and downright refuses to pay the fine, the security committee at my shared ownership development not only assesses a fine but turns the matter over to the state highway patrol, which imposes its own fines. Further, the highway patrol turns the matter over to the state judiciary system. As a result, the incident is reflected on the accused's driving record and can lead to an increase in insurance premiums.

See how much better it is to act rationally and offer a reasonable explanation?

TIP

Challenging the authority of the security or enforcement committee may seem like a good idea at the time, but usually it won't work. The committee's authority stems from the CC&Rs, the bylaws, or the incorporation documents, all of which you agreed to live by when you bought into the development. Challenging that authority is sort of like challenging the right of your hand to scratch your back.

TRAP

Refusing to pay fines imposed after due process (according to the rules of your development) can have serious consequences. A lien (if it's a condo or townhouse) or bill (if it's a co-op) might be imposed on your unit, and failure to pay can result in the loss of privileges. In some states, where an association is prevented from filing a lien for unpaid fines, it can haul you into small claims court.

What Is My Recourse If I Feel I've Been Unfairly Treated by the Committee?

Of course, the committee members may be unreasonable. They may be acting out their own power agenda and imposing demands that don't comply with the rules. Or maybe you just disagree. Either way, what can you do now? You have a variety of choices:

- Petition the full committee and ask for a review.
- Appeal the matter to the board.
- Ask for a vote of the membership.
- Go to mediation.
- Sue the board and the owners.
- Sell your property and leave.

The choices above are in descending order of severity. We'll consider each separately.

Petition the Full Committee and Ask for a Review

Frequently the initial ruling is made by only a few members of the committee. For example, you may want to change the color of a window frame and one committee member comes out and says no. But you know that the color you want to use is found on other units. So you petition the entire committee to review the matter. It may take some time, as much as a month or more, but upon review, the entire committee may see it your way—or not.

Appeal the Matter to the Board

A committee usually works under the authority of the board of directors. If you disagree with a committee ruling, you can appeal it to the board. The formal way to appeal is to call the general manager or board president and ask that the matter be brought up as an agenda item at the next regular meeting.

TIP

Sometimes the best way to make an appeal is informally. If you're friendly with one or two of the board members, give them a call. Let them know what your problem is and ask them how best to handle it. They may suggest a formal appeal to the board. Or they may simply agree to bring it up at the next meeting under "other business" and champion your cause. If this happens, you've an excellent chance of succeeding.

Assuming that you're put on the agenda, you'll have to show up at the scheduled meeting. When it's time for you to be heard, stand up and present your case. You'll need to explain the problem, the difficulty you've had in getting it resolved to your satisfaction, and, most important, what you want the board to do.

TRAP

Don't be long-winded. Board members are donating their time and consider it precious. Be succinct. Don't tell stories. Just present the facts as you believe them to be. If you have supporting documents that need to be seen, make copies and hand them out to all board members. As they say when writing an essay, state what you're going to do, do it, say what you've done, and stop.

TRAP

Don't show up with an attorney to speak for you. You want to appeal to the board members as neighbors and friends. You don't want to start off in an adversarial relationship. If you show up with an attorney who speaks for you, any smart board will simply refer the matter to its own attorney. Then, before you know it, you're into litigation (see below). You're far more likely to prevail just by showing up on your own and explaining what you want and why you think you've been wronged. Remember, you're a member too, and if at all possible, the board will try to find a way at least to compromise with you.

Assuming that the board is not dysfunctional (in which case anything can happen, from your being yelled at to your not even being allowed to speak), it will agree to consider the matter. The board may call on committee members to explain their side. The issue may be held over for future consideration. Or the board may vote.

TIP

Before you appeal to the board, find out if any of your neighbors will support you. If so, invite them to appear and speak for you. Making an appeal as a group is much more forceful than simply showing up yourself, and will command much greater board attention. The last thing the board wants is to fight a bunch of members.

Quite frankly, unless you've got very strong extenuating circumstances, the board is not likely to overrule its own committee. More than likely the board will try to find a compromise, as noted above. If one can't be found, chances are your appeal will be voted down.

Ask for a Vote of the Membership

Once the board votes you down, you're pretty much out of luck. You can, of course, bring the matter up before the board on a second appeal. But unless you have something really new and significant to present, you're not likely to change things. Now your recourse is either to accept the negative result or bump the whole thing up a level. You can ask for a vote of the membership.

TRAP

Don't expect the usual one-person, one-vote rule. Shared ownership developments aren't democracies. The voting may be apportioned according to the amount of square footage in a unit, the number of bedrooms, or some other method. Thus, while you may end up with only one vote, your neighbor could have two! Find out the voting arrangement (usually in the CC&Rs or the bylaws) for your development and then use it to your advantage. If some owners have more votes than others, try to get them on your side!

Most members forget about the vote. Not a good idea, if your goal really is to get a rule changed. It may be far easier, and cheaper, to solicit a vote of the membership. In most developments there are specific ways to obtain a membership vote.

Usually getting a vote involves having a petition signed by a minimum number of members. If you can convince that minimum to sign, you may already have won and may not even need to go to a vote. Just show up with the petition signed by a large number of members; most boards will reconsider and may even grant what you want. Boards definitely do not want a divisive vote.

On the other hand, there's nothing to say that your board will act rationally. You may have to go forward and get a vote of the members. However, be prepared for costs. You may be asked to foot the bill for the vote.

TIP

Voting may or may not bring the result you desire. In two cases I witnessed, the member who demanded the vote played the political card. That is, the vote became not only a vote on the member's cause but also a recall of one or more board members. In other words, the stakes were raised. In one case the member won; in the other she lost.

Go for Mediation

In some states, such as California, both sides are required to seek alternative dispute resolution (ADR) when their positions become intractable. Usually this takes the form of mediation or arbitration. It's not always a solution, but in many cases you must try before going to the next step. In some cases it may resolve the problem, although you may have to make considerable concessions (as with the board).

Sue the Board and the Owners

As an alternative to going to a vote (or even after an unfavorable vote) and after attempts at mediation have failed, you can take the matter to court. I do not recommend this route in any but the most extreme circumstances. There are three reasons.

First, consider the cost. Just to hire an attorney and get the
paperwork done and filed is likely to cost you $1500 to $3500. If the
board answers your suit, as it surely must, you now begin adding to
the legal bills. Another $20,000 to pursue the lawsuit to completion,
regardless of the verdict, is not unreasonable. Is your cause worth
that amount of money? (By the way, depending on your state's rules,
you may not be able to recover your legal costs even if you win.)

Second, you'll make enemies of friends. When you sue the board,
you sue every other member in the development. If you win and are
awarded damages, they could all be liable to you. This is not the way
to gain supporters. Even those who may think you've got a just cause
will begin rooting against you. Further, they're paying the cost of the
board's attorney(s). (Even if the development has insurance to pay
attorney's fees, your lawsuit could cause an increase in insurance
rates, to be paid for by higher member assessments.)

Third, you don't know that you'll win. You might. But you might
just as easily lose. If you insist on a jury trial, who knows how it could
go? Similarly, a judge may find against you.

If you feel you're in the right and that you must pursue your
cause, then by all means do. Just be aware of the cost in money,
friends, and results.

Sell Your Property and Leave

Sometimes desertion is really the best way out. If you don't like the
rules of the development (and you may be perfectly justified in not
liking them), it might be best for all, especially you, if you leave. Sell
your property or rent it out. Go elsewhere and start over. It could be
the best solution for your pocketbook, your peace of mind, and even
your health.

Is There Anything I Can Do to Prepare Myself?

Every development has its own style of operation. When you first
move in, chances are you won't have a clue as to "how things are
done." However, you can quickly get up to speed.

Make it a point of going to meetings. Get to know other owners,
committee members, and the board. Most developments offer many

social opportunities, ranging from regular parties to card games. Join in. Become one of the crowd. Very quickly you'll learn who the power brokers are. And then when you want something done, you'll know who to contact.

This is not to say that you'll get a committee or a board to go against the rules just because you've become friends with its members (although that certainly has happened). It's just to say that there's a lot of politics in shared ownership developments.

7

Special Tips and Traps When Buying a Condo

What, exactly, are you purchasing when you buy a condominium? Is it the land? Is it the floors and ceiling? Is it a small part of the entire development?

For those new to condos (and even for some who are familiar with them), shared ownership is a mystery. How, exactly does one "share" ownership with others?

What Is an Airspace?

Actually a condominium is akin to virtual reality. Now you see it, now you don't. It's a theoretical construct that lives because of legal definitions. In a physical world, however, it's existence is only a maybe.

Technically speaking, when you buy a condominium unit you are purchasing an "airspace." You get a fee simple title, which is the highest and strongest form of title, meaning that you and you alone own the property. However, the property is the distance from floor to ceiling and from wall to peripheral wall of your unit.

Be sure you understand the concept. Think of an apartment building that's three stories tall. Now think of the units on the second floor. Finally, imagine a second-floor unit smack dab in the middle of the building: unit 2G.

Unit 2G has other units with people living in them below it, on the first floor. It has other units with people living in them above it, on the third floor. And it has units with people living in them surrounding it on all sides. It is simply an airspace in the middle of a large building.

Now imagine that instead of renting unit 2G, you buy it. You buy the airspace that it represents situated in the middle of the building. That is what you own.

In addition, you get a portion of the ownership in the shared or common areas. These include the land under the building, the roof and airspace above the building, the external walls, the walkways, and all amenities such as a swimming pool and tennis court. Your ownership interest in the shared portion may amount to 1 percent or less, depending on how many owners there are. However, what you own alone remains only your airspace.

What Are the Benefits of Owning an Airspace?

We've covered the general benefits of shared ownership in Chapter 3 and elsewhere. However, there are some specific benefits to owning an airspace. To begin with, you are usually relieved of *all* external maintenance and repair concerns. Someone else takes care of mowing lawns and cleaning the pool. Someone else worries about painting the building. Most important, someone else worries about fixing the roof if repairs are needed or taking care of drainage if the basement floods. Those are not your individual responsibilities.

Another benefit is that you are literally surrounded by your neighbors. Almost all of them (except for those in rented-out units) are owners. For some people this represents a heightened level of security.

Finally, you pay less when you purchase. Today in many areas land is the single highest cost of real estate, eclipsing the cost of the building on it. Here, however, you individually don't own the land (although you own a portion of it along with all the other owners). Therefore, the cost of your unit is going to be inherently less than a piece of real estate where you alone own the land.

TRAP

Buying a condo unit is usually much cheaper than buying a single-family residence in a similar area. However, it will also bring in much less when you resell.

Apartment Building/Condominium

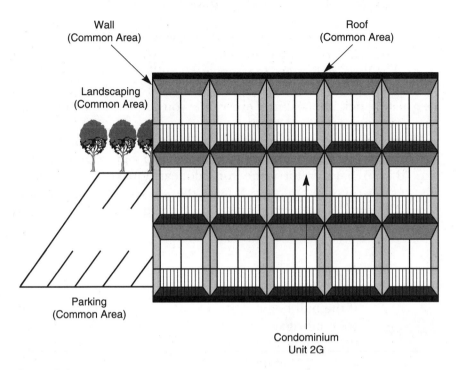

Figure 7-1.

What Are the Drawbacks of Owning an Airspace?

A condo unit will very likely be noisier than either a single-family residence or a townhouse (discussed in the next chapter). After all, you've got people living above, below, and around you. No matter how conscientious they are, there's bound to be some noise coming through to your unit.

TIP

When purchasing a condo, pay special attention to the noise insulation (as opposed to the heat insulation). Well-constructed units are almost soundproof. However, this feature usually must be built in at the time of construction. It is very difficult to retrofit it later on.

You won't have as much privacy outside your unit. You may have a porch or deck, for example. But chances are your neighbors' porch or deck will be right next to yours and you'll be able to see them when you're on it, just as they'll be able to see you. Similarly, you'll be greeting neighbors almost every time you come into the building and go in and out of your unit.

In the event of a catastrophe, you could lose everything. This drawback is seldom considered by those who buy condos, but it should be. What if a hurricane, tornado, earthquake, fire, or other disaster destroys the building? Where, then, is your airspace on the second floor (2G) located? With the building gone, it no longer exists.

TRAP

If the building is destroyed, you may not be relieved of your mortgage payments. Unless you have insurance that specifically covers the cause of the destruction, the mortgage company will not be paid off and will seek to collect, even if your airspace no longer exists!

Can I Buy Insurance to Cover All Risks?

You probably can't buy insurance on your own, although the HOA (homeowners association) may be able to. For example, if you live on the West Coast your building may be in jeopardy from earthquakes. Naturally you would want to buy earthquake insurance.

However, insurance companies are not going to be eager to sell it to you. Indeed, at different times in California, areas that are likely to be hit by quakes have not been able to obtain earthquake insurance at any cost.

Further, as an individual airspace owner, you probably do not have an insurable loss. After all, if there's a quake, how can an insurance company guarantee to rebuild your airspace without reconstructing the entire building?

This is why the HOA will often try to take out the insurance. The homeowners as a group may be able to purchase a policy that covers the entire building, including your unit. However, because of the likely risk of loss in earthquake country, the cost of the policy will surely be high and there will be a high deductible as well as many exclusions.

TRAP

 Because of the high cost, many HOAs refuse to spend the money on insurance. Rather than raise the dues of each member $50, $100, or more per month, they simply forgo the high-risk insurance. No problem—unless and until an earthquake, flood, hurricane, or other disaster hits. (*Note:* Some CC&Rs *require* the association to purchase disaster insurance.)

If There Is Insurance, Will I Be Covered?

Maybe. Maybe not. It depends on how good the insurance is. Many HOAs boast of their insurance coverage. Yet they may not have enough insurance to cover replacement of the entire building.

TIP

 Be sure to find out what insurance your development has and have a competent insurance agent check it out, especially your deductible

Remember, it doesn't take much to make a large building uninhabitable. An earthquake or hurricane knocking part of the structure off its foundation can cause the entire building to be condemned by local authorities. Your particular unit may be unaffected. But you could be prevented from occupying it because of a problem with the overall structure. (Even a fire to one part of a building may make the entire building uninhabitable.)

Further, if the building is destroyed, will there be a consensus on replacing it? If the insurance coverage is complete, then the insuring company will probably take over the job of replacement and may even find you a place to live during reconstruction. However, if the coverage turns out not to be complete—perhaps there is a high deductible—it's a different story. Each owner may now have to come up with many thousands of dollars for reconstruction.

Whenever individual owners need to provide money to reconstruct the building, reactions differ. Some owners are ready to go, others can't raise the money, and still others want the building rebuilt differently. In short, even if the association can raise the needed funds through assessments or through a new mortgage, there will still be a debate over how to proceed. I have seen such arguments perilously prolonged. Ten years after the catastrophe, the building still has not been replaced and the owners are in court fighting each other over what to do. Needless to say in such a situation your investment is gravely jeopardized.

TIP

You should be able to purchase insurance to cover at least your belongings. Although this won't help with your real estate investment, it could help you get started again elsewhere.

What Other Specific Concerns Should I Have About a Condo?

In Chapter 2 and elsewhere we covered concerns such as density, noise, location within the development, and the layout of the unit itself. There are several other concerns specific to condos that you also need to consider.

What Are My Personal-Use Facilities?

You own only your unit individually. At the same time, you may have sole access to parts of the condominium development that are owned in common. Consider the garage. Some developments have underground parking or parking in an aboveground structure. Others have designated covered parking areas in a lot. Still others have exposed parking. (A lot depends on what part of the country you live in and the type of weather in that area.)

You may have a designated parking spot that only you can use. You may not own it individually. Instead it's owned by everyone as part of the common area. But as long as you own your condo unit, only you will have access to that parking spot.

TRAP

Be wary of failing to pay your condominium assessment. The HOA can usually put a lien on your property and even force a sale to recover back dues, though such an extreme step is rarely taken. Rather, your "privileges" are likely to be revoked if you don't pay what you owe promptly. For example, you could find someone else occupying your parking spot until you pay up! (Some developments specify certain parking spaces for units in the CC&Rs or bylaws and these cannot be taken away.)

Other areas that may belong to all the owners in common but that only you have access to include:

- A deck or balcony adjacent to your unit
- A garden area adjacent to your unit
- A gate that leads exclusively to your unit

What About Property Taxes?

As the individual owner of a condominium unit, you will be required to pay property taxes. Your responsibility is the same as if you owned a single-family detached home.

The taxes are based on an appraisal of the property's value and are assessed according to the rules of each state. The appraisal may be based on the purchase price or construction cost, or it may be based on a regular evaluation done every few years. Some states impose a high tax rate while others impose a lower one.

Your taxes usually will be assessed at the end of June and will come due twice yearly, typically in early December and early March. How you pay them usually depends on the arrangement made with your mortgage lender. If your mortgage is for 80 percent of the purchase price or less, you will be given the option of paying the taxes yourself when they come due. If your mortgage is for a higher percentage of loan to value, you will usually be required to pay one-twelfth of the taxes each month into an impound account managed by the lender. From this account the lender will then pay your taxes twice a year when they come due.

The penalty for failure to pay taxes will vary from state to state. Most states wait a period of time, typically three to five years, and then sell your property for back taxes. However, failure to pay taxes is cause for foreclosure in virtually all mortgage documents. Foreclosure protects the collateral for the loan. So if you have a mortgage, the lender will begin foreclosure long before the state moves in.

What About Utility Bills?

Utilities present a mixed bag. It all depends on how the building was constructed. Most modern buildings have separate utility meters for every unit. That means that you will probably have to pay separate bills for:

Water

Gas

Electric

Cable TV

On the other hand, in some developments the HOA pays "bulk rates" for certain utilities and then recovers the cost from the general dues. Utilities paid for in common may include:

Garbage collection

Cable TV

Water

Fuel oil (for heating)

Note that there is an overlap. It all depends on how your development is set up. Rest assured, however, that whether you pay utility costs through general dues or through individual bills for your unit, you'll be charged for all services.

What About Laundry Facility Arrangements?

In modern condo units, there is usually a laundry room or at least a laundry area within your unit where you can hook up a washer and dryer. (In some cases both gas and electric outlets will be provided; in other cases only electric outlets may be available.)

However, in older units or units that were converted from apartments (see Chapter 10) washer and dryer facilities may not have been built into each unit. If that's the case, you may be *required* to use a common laundry room.

By required I don't mean that anyone will prevent you from taking your laundry to an outside laundrette or cleaners. I mean that you may be prohibited from installing a washer and dryer in your own facility, which is what many owners will want to do.

The problem is usually one of drainage and construction. There may not be a drain in the right place to accommodate a washing machine and to install one would require breaking through walls in other owners' apartments, a big no-no. Similarly, bulkier construction of walls and floors is usually required to handle the vibrations from a washing machine and dryer. Simply to put these appliances in a closet and turn them on might give your neighbor-owners the shakes!

Thus, in a building where washing facilities are not built into each unit, don't expect to be able to put them in yourself. Unless the association specifically permits it, you probably won't be allowed.

How Far Away Is Your Car?

Finally, there's the matter of the distance between your unit and your parking space. Assuming you don't have a garage right next to your unit, you're going to have to park in a central area and then walk some distance. The trick can be particularly annoying when you're carrying groceries or other heavy items.

Consequently, owners clamor to have their parking space as close to their unit as possible. Often a condo plan will identify a parking spot as being for the exclusive use of a particular unit. For example, unit 1 must use parking spot 1. This avoids confrontation. Where the HOA has flexibility in assigning parking spots, it will usually make an effort to accommodate everyone, but many owners will still be required to walk a greater distance than they would like. And the only way to get closer is to move someone else farther away.

Two negatives can result. First, there may be constant feuding over parking locations. Second, the value of a unit may be reduced because of a distant parking space. The unit will simply be harder to sell. It's something to think about.

Is a Condo a Safe Investment?

In an age when investors seem willing to throw money at speculative stocks that have virtually no near-term earnings potential, it may seem incongruous to worry about how risky a condo investment may be. However, it should be a concern for new buyers as well as current owners. Will your unit hold its value over time? Will you be able to resell for a profit?

Generally speaking, condos follow the overall real estate market in your area. Barring some catastrophe (see Chapter 4), the value of your unit should increase, remain fairly constant, or decrease with the overall market.

Of course, you also need to consider the peculiarities of shared ownership. How well the HOA runs things, whether or not there are lawsuits, how the overall neighborhood fares (whether it declines or gets better), and so on will also affect value.

In short, a well-located, well-designed condo (see Chapter 2 on evaluating a particular unit) is probably as good an investment as any other real estate. Just realize that there are no guarantees. Changing conditions in the market, within the neighborhood, within the association, and elsewhere could affect your investment.

Remember, no investment—and that includes stocks, bonds, and real estate—always appreciates. We can hope for our investments to go up most of the time. But they also could go down.

8

Special Tips and Traps When Buying a Townhouse

For most people the distinction between a townhouse and a condo comes down to more land and more room in the townhouse. This usually is very true. In fact, the term "townhouse" is basically not a legal distinction, but rather a term used to describe an architectural design.

What Is a Townhouse?

Typically with a townhouse you don't have people above you or below you. You might only have attached neighbors at the side. There may be a roof above your unit and either a basement or garage below. And you probably have a garden or patio area out back. As opposed to the airspace of a condo, you have a kind of groundspace in a townhouse.

In a very real sense, a townhouse is a compromise between a single-family dwelling and a typical condo. It usually gives you some land. On the other hand, you also usually share walls with your neighbors.

Be sure you understand this latter. Townhomes usually share walls; thus they have less land than single-family detached homes, which have open land on all four sides. A typical townhouse may have just as much square footage inside as a typical single-family detached home. However, it may only occupy half as much land.

Is a Townhouse Technically a Condo?

It can be. As described in the last chapter, it may be a condo development, just with a much roomier design.

On the other hand, a townhouse more often is one unit of a PUD or Planned Unit Development. A PUD differs from a condominium development in several important ways.

You'll recall that in a condo, you only own an airspace, a piece of virtual property. With a PUD you not only own the airspace which your unit occupies, but also the land beneath and the air above. You do, however, have mutual walls with your neighbors and there are common areas, such as walkways, driveways, swimming pools, and so on shared with other owners.

A townhouse could also be a co-op, although that is rare. See Chapter 9 for more on co-ops.

TIP

Don't assume that any property with units all on the ground floor is a PUD. I have seen condominium developments with only one level. It looked exactly like a PUD development, only it wasn't. The distinction comes from how the development was originally planned, not in the way it looks.

How Is Title Held?

Whether it's a condominium or a PUD, you get fee simple or full title to your property. As we've discussed, for a condo that means an airspace, for a PUD that includes the land directly underneath your unit. In both cases, however, it also includes areas held in common. This may involve gardens, paths, and other areas that come right up to your front and back doors.

PLANNED COMMUNITY/TOWNHOUSES

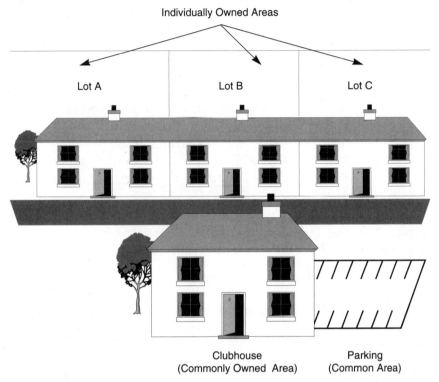

Figure 8-1.

Usually the garages and walkways attached to individual townhouse units are included in the title. However, that may not be the case. Check your deed carefully. If you're not sure how to read it, consult a good real estate agent or an attorney to see exactly what areas it covers. (A title insurance officer may be able to let you know as well.)

What Is the Structure of a PUD?

Just as in a condominium, there are CC&Rs that define the land usage. The common areas are administered by a homeowners association (HOA), which is guided by the bylaws. The PUD is run by a board of directors. There may be a general manager (often an outside contractor), a variety of committees, regular meetings, and so on. The management structure is virtually identical to that of a condo development. Check out Chapter 7 for more details.

TIP

As with a condo, you should carefully read the CC&Rs and the bylaws (as well as any rules passed by the board) to see if you'd like living in the townhouse. You may find that while you like the overall layout of the development, you find the rules overbearing.

What Are the Advantages of a Townhouse?

There are many advantages of a townhouse. We'll look at several. However, keep in mind that each development is different. Indeed, as noted earlier, some condos are actually set up like townhouses. Thus while the following advantages apply to most townhouse developments, they don't apply to all.

Increased Privacy. In a typical condominium you're likely to have neighbors on all sides as well as above and below. On the other hand, in a townhouse, your neighbors are limited to those on either side. Because of the lower density, there's increased privacy. In addition, townhouse units often have their own garden and lawn areas, both in front and in back, something seldom found in condos.

Bigger Units. Townhouses are typically bigger than condos. This, however, is not a hard-and-fast rule, since some condos are quite large. Because townhouse developments are structured horizontally rather than vertically, they occupy more land than a typical condo development. To justify the increased cost of the land, bigger units are usually put up. Thus, while it's common to find condos starting at 600 to 700 square feet, it's rare to find a townhouse with less than 1000 square feet, and a typical unit is much larger.

TIP

Individual townhouse units can be several stories tall. I've seen many that have three levels. However, you own all the levels.

Less Noise. Fewer units (lower density) means fewer neighbors and that usually translates into less noise. That doesn't mean that a particular unit might not have extra noise coming from the street or the swimming pool or some other area. However, in general townhouses are quieter than condos.

Garages and Utility Rooms. While some condos have individual garages and utility rooms for washer and dryer, many do not. On the other hand, it's a very unusual townhouse that doesn't have these features. Typically the garage is either directly attached to the unit or connected by means of a short walkway. Either way, it's your garage, one you don't have to share with neighbors.

More Open Space. Since townhouses are all "on the ground," so to speak, the developments tend to be more spread out, with a substantial amount of common area. As a result, there are more walkways, greenbelts, and open areas.

In many parts of the country, almost all single-family homes are fenced. While that adds to privacy, it detracts from an open, spacious feeling.

By contrast, even though a townhouse may have a tiny fenced-in court or patio area, typically the area between units is open, giving an airy feeling. Thus, you often get the feeling that a townhouse has more outside room than a single-family home.

Better Layouts. Because they are typically bigger than condos and have no units above or below them, townhouses often have a better layout. Even though most units have two walls in common with neighbors, they may be designed with skylights to bring in additional light or with different levels of floors to break up the space. End units may have additional windows.

TIP

The most preferred townhouse units are on the end and, thus, share only one wall instead of two. The extra free wall allows for more window space and eliminates "through-wall noise." Some townhouses are built as duplexes, two units side by side, with only one shared wall each. In such premium developments, everyone gets to have an end unit!

What Questions Should I Ask When Buying a Townhouse?

Of course, you'll want to ask all the questions we've talked about earlier in the book with regard to shared ownership developments. You want to look at the CC&Rs, the bylaws, and the rules. (Reread Chapter 4 if you're not sure of what to look for.) In addition, there are a few other items that should be of concern to you.

Who Is Responsible for the Roof?

In a condo, where you own only your airspace, the roof is usually the concern of all the owners in the development. It is repaired and replaced by the homeowners association.

In a townhouse, on the other hand, you typically have a roof above your unit. That means that it could be up to you alone to maintain, repair, and replace the roof. Be sure to check the CC&Rs, which will spell this out. The last thing you want is to buy a townhouse thinking the HOA will take care of everything, only to discover that you must come up with thousands of dollars to fix the roof.

Who Is Responsible for the Lawn, Garden, Deck, or Patio?

In a condo, usually everything outside your airspace is the responsibility of the homeowners association. Not so in a townhouse development. You could be responsible for watering, planting, and maintaining gardens, shrubs, bushes, and lawns in the front and rear of your unit. You could be responsible for maintaining and repairing a deck or patio that abuts your unit.

As with the roof, you need to find out *before* you make a purchase. That way if something is wrong, you can ask the seller to take care of it before you buy. Also, you'll be aware of what extra costs and work are involved.

TIP

 When you purchase, you should get a copy of the title report, including a map of the development as well as the location of your unit. You should also be given documents that spell out which areas belong to the HOA and which belong to you. Take the time to read them carefully.

What If I Want to Put in My Own Swimming Pool or Spa?

As a practical matter, most townhouses simply don't have enough outside area for a swimming pool. But they frequently do have enough area for a spa.

Assuming there are no specific rules against it, will the HOA let you put one in? The answer could be yes, particularly if the spa can be installed without being visible from other units or common areas. (A good place is a walled-in area between the garage and the home itself.)

You will, of course, still need to get the customary building permits and probably permission from the HOA. But permission for a spa (or similar enclosure) is far easier to obtain in a townhouse than in a condo.

Is a View Important?

A home with a view always commands a higher price than a home without. That's true of single-family detached dwellings, condos, co-ops, and townhouses. However, townhouse units with a view command a significantly higher price than neighboring units without.

An important consideration, of course, is what the view is of. If it's of the swimming pool, because you live right next to it, the view can actually be a drawback. During the summer months you'll be seeing people swimming and hearing noise from the pool.

On the other hand, if it's a view of the mountains, a lake, or the sea, that vista could make a big difference in price. In many townhouse developments, units on the view side of the street cost almost twice as much as those on the other (no-view) side.

Is It Easy to Get Financing on a Townhouse?

It's certainly no harder than financing a typical condo. And if yours happens to be a PUD, it can be considerably easier. While lenders are often concerned about (and suspicious of) how well a typical condo association is run, they have fewer misgivings with PUDs. That's because of the fact that there's land underneath the airspace and a lower population density. (With co-ops, by contrast, financing can be more difficult to obtain. See Chapter 9.)

You can choose from an array of financing arrangements—from very low down payment loans to adjustable-rate or fixed-rate mortgages to anything else available in the residential market. PUDs are suitable for "conforming loans" or financing that is underwritten by Fannie Mae, Freddie Mac, or a similar mortgage pool. In short, they command the lowest rates and best loans around.

What About Insurance?

You should be able to get fire and liability insurance as easily as you can with a single-family detached home. However, as discussed in other chapters, it may be more difficult to obtain specialty insurance—for earthquakes, floods, hurricanes, or other disasters. Because of the attached nature of the structure, many insurers will only issue policies covering the entire development. That means the HOA will have to get the specialty insurance.

Do I Pay My Own Taxes?

If it's technically a condo or a PUD, it is taxed in exactly the same way as a single-family detached house. You own your own property and you'll get a tax bill requiring payment, usually twice a year. (You may never see a tax bill if your taxes are part of your mortgage payment—the lender takes care of paying the bill.)

Also, if you sell for a profit, just as with a house, you will be subject to capital gains tax. If it's your residence, you may be able to take advantage of the one-time exclusion (up to $250,000) provided to those who sell their main home and meet other qualifications.

Is a Townhouse a Better Deal?

Most people think the townhouse is innately better in concept than the typical condo or the co-op. As a result, townhouses cost significantly more, as a rule, than either of the other two. Of course, a lot depends on location, amenities, condition, the HOA, and so forth. And a lot depends on how much you are willing and able to pay.

9

Special Tips and Traps When Buying a Co-op

A co-op is not a condo and a condo is not a co-op. Although they may physically look similar, the ownership structure is quite different. Many of the rules and conditions under which owners live are different too.

What Is a Co-op?

A cooperative is basically a corporation formed to hold real estate—in this case, a specific property. The corporation builds a cooperative dwelling—or more likely, buys an existing apartment (rental) building and converts it—and then offers shares of stock. When you buy a co-op, you purchase those shares of stock and then get a proprietary lease to an apartment. The lease is frequently for 99 years and almost always has an option for renewal.

Frequently the first owners of conversions are the "tenants in possession"—renters who are asked if they want to buy the apartment unit in which they live.

TIP

Most states have laws that give "tenants in possession" the right to remain as tenants after the co-op has been converted and, in some cases, even to renew their lease. The exception is when a large percentage of tenants (usually two-thirds or more) want to convert. An "eviction plan" (rather than individual eviction procedures) is then put into effect to remove nonbuying tenants over a period of time.

TIP

Buying into a co-op on the East Coast is frequently called buying an apartment. On the West Coast and in much of the rest of the country, the word "apartment" usually refers only to a rental. Actually, an apartment means a dwelling, whether owned or rented, so buying an apartment is an accurate turn of phrase.

It's important to understand the ownership difference between a condo and a co-op. With a condo you get title to the property; you actually own airspace (or in the case of a PUD, the ground beneath and the air above as well). You get a fee simple or absolute title.

With a co-op you do not get title to any real estate. Indeed, you do not own the real estate; the corporation does. With a co-op you get stock in the corporation that owns the real estate, and that stock entitles you to a proprietary lease on a specified apartment from the corporation. You're a stockholder and a tenant, not a property owner.

TRAP

Remember, when you buy a co-op, you don't actually own your apartment. You're renting it from the corporation, in which you have ownership as evidenced by stock.

What Are the Advantages of Buying a Co-op?

There are some enormous advantages to owning a co-op, as well as some distinct disadvantages. We'll consider the pluses first.

DIFFERENCES BETWEEN CONDO/TOWNHOUSES AND CO-OPS

CONDO/TOWNHOUSES

- You get a deed and title to your "airspace."
- Financing is often easier.
- Your assessment is lower.
- You pay your own mortgage and taxes.
- You can't be evicted, but you can be foreclosed.
- You need only deal with the seller, when buying.
- You need only deal with the buyer, when selling.
- Almost always you can rent out your unit.

CO-OPS

- You get shares of stock in the co-op corporation.
- You get a lease to your "apartment."
- Your monthly "fees" are often high to cover an underlying mortgage, taxes, and other costs.
- You can be evicted.
- Your shares of stock can be sold out from under you in certain circumstances.
- You must often win board approval to buy in.
- You must often get board approval of the new buyer to resell.
- You may *not* be able to rent out your unit easily.

Big Profits, in Some Cases

Some owners of co-ops have seen enormous price increases in their shares and, consequently, huge profits. However, it is a mistake to think that this is a common or guaranteed occurrence.

Most of the big gains have occurred as a result of an apartment building in an urban area (such as Manhattan) converting to co-op status. The first owners (often the former tenants) realize huge increases when they resell—in large part because of the shortage of available rentals. They own an apartment in a city where just finding any place to live can be a problem.

Another factor has been timing. Most co-ops were established a good many years ago, before the big price hikes in real estate that occurred in the late 1970s, the late 1980s, and once again in the late 1990s. Many early co-op owners have benefited (on paper) from these market bumps. For those who bought co-ops in urban areas where there were already housing shortages (as noted above), the increases have been especially dramatic. Generally, if you buy during an economic downturn, just prior to a market surge, you stand to see a sizable increase in the value of your investment, regardless of the type of shared ownership.

TRAP

Of course, if you buy during an up period when the market is booming, as in the late 1990s, you're likely to see the value of your unit decline later on. As noted, timing is everything.

Lower Price to Get In

Frequently the cost of buying a co-op is significantly less than buying a single-family home in the same area. Sometimes, for factors discussed below, it is even much less than for buying a comparable condo in the area. This does not, however, mean that a co-op is cheap. In New York City, for example, a three-bedroom co-op apartment with only 1500 square feet of space could easily sell for $600,000 or more.

Of course, those same factors that allow you to buy a co-op for a lower price initially will usually come back to haunt you when it's time to sell. At resale time you won't be able to command as high a price as you could for other types of real estate.

TIP

Location is critical. In some urban settings the *only* type of housing that's available is a co-op. In that case the price may be astronomical both when you buy and when you sell.

You Get Shared Ownership Benefits

Like a condo, a co-op offers you the benefits of shared ownership. What you do inside your apartment is largely up to you (although you could be restricted in structural changes and/or changes that affect other owners). The corporation takes care of all the outside or common areas—for example, hallways, garages, the staffing of doormen and/or garage attendants, and the overall structure.

Many co-ops set aside areas for meetings or social events. There may be a gymnasium, swimming pool, spa, and other amenities, all of which you can participate in because you are a stockholder in the corporation.

What Are the Big Disadvantages?

The key disadvantages to any form of shared ownership have been noted in earlier chapters. They include:

- Loss of privacy due to increased density
- More noise than a single-family home
- Loss of control

Two other areas of concern—financial stability and resale—are peculiar to the ownership structure of a co-op.

Is a Co-op Financially Stable?

By its very nature a co-op is less financially stable than a condo. Remember, when you buy into a condo, you own your unit. If you can't make the payments on your mortgage, you lose, not the other owners. (They lose only the fees that you would otherwise pay toward the upkeep of the common areas.)

With a co-op, however, the corporation usually holds an underlying mortgage on the overall structure. That means that if you can't make your monthly payments to cover your portion of the building debt, the other owners must make up what you can't pay in order to meet the monthly mortgage payment. The same holds true for property taxes and insurance. If too many owners can't pay, then the remainder may not be able to make up the difference—and the entire project could go into foreclosure.

In short, a co-op arrangement is very much like an extended family with brothers, sisters, aunts, and uncles all living in close proximity and all contributing to the living expenses. When one (or more) loses a job or gets sick and can't contribute his or her share, the others must take up the slack. If they can't make it up, they could lose their home.

The inherent financial instability is the reason that good co-op boards are very careful about whom they will allow to buy stock. They want to be sure that any new owners are financially strong.

Is a Co-op Difficult to Resell?

Compared with a condo or a townhouse, a co-op can be more difficult to resell. The reasons are twofold. First, because of the strict financial requirements that the board may impose on new owners (discussed above), you may have trouble finding buyers who are qualified. Second, and more important, even a promising buyer may have difficulty getting financing.

Is It Difficult to Get Financing for a Co-op?

Remember, when you buy a co-op, you own stock, not airspace or land. Hence, your only collateral is that stock and your proprietary lease. Thus, while you can put up the property as collateral, you can't get a true mortgage.

Also, the underlying mortgage on the building, held by the co-op corporation, usually comes first in the event of a default. Thus, any stock and proprietary lease loan that a buyer might obtain is placed in a secondary position. In the event of foreclosure and forced sale, the building mortgage usually will get paid off before the stock loan on any individual unit.

TIP

When the co-op development obtains a mortgage on the building (for the common areas), it will usually try to get the lender to subordinate that mortgage to the shareholders and to limit its remedies in the event of a default. If it succeeds, then when you borrow on your unit, your lender may be able to get a more secure position. Your lender may get some rights to your apartment, but not to the building itself.

As a result, many lenders are very hesitant to make loans to individuals purchasing into a stock cooperative. In some areas of the country, that type of financing can be very difficult if not impossible to obtain.

TIP

If you're looking for co-op financing, try the National Cooperative Bank, 1401 Eye St., NW, Suite 700, Washington, DC 20005, 800-322-1251. It is experienced in co-op loans and claims it will make loans all across the country. It offers fixed-rate and adjustable loans up to 30 years at competitive interest rates and at lower settlement (closing) costs than for condos.

Why Aren't There Many Co-ops Outside the East Coast?

In New York State there are literally thousands of co-op buildings. In California there are only a few dozen. Indeed, outside of a few states on the East Coast, co-ops are a rare sight in the country.

On the other hand, condo and townhouse developments are all over the United States, including the eastern seaboard. Indeed, there are probably 100 or more condo/townhouse developments for every co-op. Some records suggest that condos existed as far back as the time of the Romans!

The reason for the disparity goes back to financing. On the East Coast, where co-ops have been around for a very long time, lenders are familiar with the arrangement and are set up to handle the specialized financing. For most of the rest of the country, however, lenders are set up only to handle mortgage financing on real estate. Thus, if you want to buy a co-op in California, for example, you'll have to spend a great deal of time trying to find any lender who will finance your purchase and you may ultimately be unsuccessful. I know, I've tried!

Can I Get Financing on My Co-op Purchase?

Yes, you can, particularly if you're in a market where co-ops are common, as on the East Coast. The financing, however, is substantially different from that on owned real estate.

Remember, when you buy a co-op, you purchase stock in a corporation that owns your unit; you have possession only on the basis of the proprietary lease. Therefore, in order to finance your purchase (get a loan for a portion of the seller's equity), you must pledge your stock as collateral. (The bank may get a security interest in the form of a chattel mortgage.)

TRAP

Because of the perils of lending on a co-op, you can expect to pay a slightly higher interest rate (and points) when you borrow, although your closing costs could be lower.

The actual details of the financing are quite complex and involve your allowing the lender to sell your stock (and evict you from the premises) should you fail to make your monthly payments. Lenders familiar with co-op loans have all the paperwork set up and know exactly how to handle the transaction.

TIP

While exact statistics are not available, probably less than 15 percent of condo and townhouse buyers pay cash for their unit (with no or little financing involved). However, that number jumps to over 50 percent with co-op buyers. Thus, when it comes time to resell your co-op, you'll be looking at a much smaller pool of potential buyers: those who have cash.

Are Most Co-ops Conversions?

With the possible exception of co-ops in New York State, most are conversions. It's rare that a developer will go out, buy land, and then form a co-op to put up a building. On the other hand, most condos and planned unit developments (PUDs) are built from the ground up.

The typical co-op begins its life cycle as an apartment building, usually in an urban setting. The building rents out for a number of years (sometimes decades), during which time it may be bought and sold by different owners, always as an apartment building.

Then, a time comes when the current owner discovers that there is far more profit to be made in selling the property as a cooperative rather than as an apartment building. This is because the value of a co-op unit is based on residential real estate prices, whereas the value of an apartment is determined by the rents it brings in. For example, if an apartment building brings in rentals of $100,000 a year, its value might be 10 times that—as determined by market conditions—or $1 million. (Rental income may be limited by any number of factors, from the ability of tenants to pay to rent controls and other restrictions.)

On the other hand, by breaking up the apartment building and selling off the individual units, the owner is no longer limited by rental income. Rather, the price is determined by residential real estate valuations. Sometimes an apartment building that commands a $1 million price tag as a rental development might command $4 million or more when broken up into cooperative units. It's easy to see why so many apartment house owners have converted.

TRAP

In areas where rent controls are still in effect, conversion may not be possible until the rent controls have been lifted. However, once they are removed, conversion often takes place rapidly.

Are There Any Problems With Buying Co-op Conversions?

There can be. We'll look into conversion concerns in general in the next chapter. Here let's go over a few problems that are specific to co-op conversions.

The big problem is that co-op conversions tend to involve very old buildings. (Most condo conversions are in relatively newer structures.) That means that there may be problems involving structure and obsolescence.

Any building that is more than 30 years old raises concerns about overall structure. That concern increases as the building's age goes up. A thorough inspection of the property should include the following.

Foundation: Is It Still Sound?   Was the foundation built to modern standards? Many older foundations were built with wood (which will deteriorate) on mud sills or use bricks and stone instead of concrete. After many years these can become unstable.

Structure: Are the Beams Still in Good Shape?   Wood that is kept dry and free from pests can last centuries. However, wood that is infested with fungus, colonized by termites, or allowed to get wet can deteriorate very rapidly.

Systems: Are the Electrical, Heating, and Plumbing Systems in Good Shape?   Plumbing and wiring in older buildings may be inadequate for modern demands. You may not be able to hook up a washer and dryer because there's no drain or because the electrical lines are inadequate (no 220-volt service). You may need to depend on heat from an old boiler in the basement instead of from individual heaters in each unit.

Obsolescence: Is It Out of Date?   Your older co-op unit may only have one bathroom and it may be virtually impossible to add another. It may have little to no insulation in the walls to reduce heat loss or noise. It may have a small, old-fashioned kitchen that is difficult or impossible to remodel. Remember, remodeling an old house is quite different from remodeling an old apartment. With the house, you can break through and make changes as you wish. With the apartment, you must cater to the demands of the board and the other owners.

How Hard Is It to Buy Into a Co-op?

Success in buying into a co-op depends on whether you qualify. We've already discussed some of the problems that could crop up with financing. Now let's turn to another issue: Will the board of residents sell you shares of stock?

Unlike the owners of a condo or townhouse, the owners of a co-op unit can't really sell you that unit. Remember, they don't own it. Rather, what the owners can do is sell you shares of stock in the cooperative. However, that means that the cooperative must issue new shares in your name, something it may or may not be willing to do. In some co-op buildings the board *must* issue new stock to new owners. In most cases, however, the board may do so at its own discretion.

Today federal laws prohibit discrimination on the basis of race, religion, and national origin. However, the cooperative may be restrictive in other ways, primarily financial. It's worth noting that former President Richard Nixon was rejected when he applied to purchase a unit in a prestigious New York co-op. The reason? The owners reportedly did not want their building associated with notoriety. The same has happened to entertainers.

You probably will be required to appear before the board of directors/residents (or a membership committee). You probably will be asked to present income tax returns, bank statements, profit and loss statements (if you own a business), verifications of employment, and so on.

In addition, you may be asked questions about the number of people who will occupy the unit (there may be a limit on occupancy), whether you will have a water bed (which may be prohibited because of obvious concerns), whether you're a smoker (if the entire building is smoke free), what your age is (if it's a seniors-only building), and so on.

TIP

It's always a good idea to put your best foot forward when appearing before the board or membership committee. Don't be argumentative or challenging of authority. Try to persuade, not demand.

In fairness (and to protect itself from charges of discrimination) the board or membership committee will most likely have a list of qualifications that each new owner must satisfy. Usually, it will try to apply those qualifications fairly.

However, undoubtedly your reviewers also will be sizing you up to see how well you fit with the existing owners. As a practical matter, given two equally qualified would-be buyers (as is sometimes the case in a strong market), it may come down to who the board or membership committee likes the most. In some cases a board will give no reason for declining a prospective owner.

Why Are Co-op Fees So High?

While the monthly fees for a condo or townhouse development are typically in the range of a few hundred dollars, the "rent" for a co-op may be in the thousands of dollars. Why the difference?

It's because the co-op fees frequently include a mortgage payment (on the underlying mortgage covering the entire structure), tax payment, insurance, and sometimes utilities. Yes, your payment could be very high. But it also could cover a great deal more than fees for a condo or townhouse.

Can the Board Keep Me From Renting Out My Co-op?

Yes, it probably can. If the Board adopts rules against renting or subletting units, you could be out of luck. In fact, there very likely will be a clause in your lease or purchase agreement that prohibits or restricts rentals.

TIP

 Because of the complicated rules involved in co-ops, check them out carefully. It's also a good idea to have an attorney familiar with this type of development look over all documents before you sign.

Not being able to rent out your unit may not seem like such a big deal when you're buying. However, it could have grave consequences later on. Say that you buy the unit and several years later discover you must move out of the area. Or you run into some financial trouble and need to move to a smaller apartment.

The obvious solution in either case is to sell. But you may not be able to sell (or want to sell) at the time. You may want to keep your unit. However, to obtain the money necessary to continue paying the fees, you need to rent it out. You put up a "For Rent" sign only to have someone from the board inform you that subletting or renting out the unit is prohibited. Suddenly you're faced with a big loss because you can't rent.

Can the Board Determine to Whom I Can Sell My Unit?

Yes, in many cases. If the board has the power to control the stock, then it effectively exerts a veto over future buyers of your unit.

Let's say you find someone who you think is ready, willing, and able to buy. Then, as noted above, your buyer appears before the board and for some reason is turned down. The board has effectively kept you from selling your unit.

As a practical matter, if someone wants to buy the unit for cash (for your equity) and is eminently qualified, it's doubtful the board will turn the offer down. But if, as is often the case, the buyer turns out to be marginal, the board may keep you from selling. It's something to consider before you buy.

Are There Any Special Rules?

Every co-op has its own rules. There could be rules against having dogs on the property, even though cats are allowed. (Dogs bark, cats don't.)

There may be rules against having any parties on weekdays, or on weekends after 10 p.m. There could be rules against almost anything.

Remember, a co-op is a much more closely knit family than a condo or townhouse. And the board, because it frequently controls the stock, has much more power.

Can I Be Evicted?

You certainly can be evicted, but not without cause. The most common reason for eviction is failure to pay your monthly fees. Remember, if you don't pay your fees, they must be made up by the other owners. Your failure to pay puts the whole development at risk.

Thus, if you don't pay for several months, you may find that, like a tenant, you're facing eviction from "your" unit. Usually at that time the board will put your shares up for sale and will accept the next qualified person who comes along. There's no guarantee that you'll get all or even any of your equity returned in such a sale.

This is added reason for you to keep current on your co-op fees. Unlike mortgage lenders on a condo or townhouse, who often find lengthy foreclosure to be the only option when owners fail to meet payments, co-op boards can act quickly.

Can My Ownership Stock Be Sold Against My Will?

Yes. As noted above, failure to pay your fees could constitute a reason to evict you. Once you are evicted, the board could lease out your unit to someone else until, ultimately, it finds a buyer for your shares—all against your will.

TRAP

It's important to keep in mind that your financial health is what allows you to live in a co-op. However, financial health can change unexpectedly. You could be in an auto accident or get sick and be unable to work. Without your income, you could be unable to pay your co-op fees. Eviction and loss of your unit can happen much more quickly in a co-op than in a condo or townhouse development.

Theoretically, you could also be sold out if you repeatedly and grossly break the rules of the board. However, this is an extreme result. More likely you'd be lectured to or fined.

Will I Be Able to Vote?

In matters that come up for a vote, you'll be able to cast your ballot along with everyone else. However, the strength of your ballot may or may not depend on the number of shares you own. Others who have bigger units, better-located units, or some other "advantage" may or may not have the same vote as you. Check it out before you buy.

Is the Board of Directors All-Powerful?

The board may seem invincible at times. When you're buying in, when you come up against the rules, or when you want to sell, it feels like the board's sole purpose is to get in your way.

However, it's important to remember that the board is made up of other owners who are trying to achieve a quality of life that most people in the development want. They are there to protect the development and the other owners. They may seem unfeeling or vindictive at times, but in the vast majority of instances they're doing what they think is best for all.

Both to protect yourself as well as to protect the development, you may want to join the board yourself. Certainly doing so will give you a sense of control over your destiny within the development. For a better picture of how boards are run, check into Chapter 5.

Will I Be Able to Deduct Interest and Taxes?

Generally speaking, all homeowners can deduct the interest on their mortgage (up to very high limits) and property taxes. But remember, as a shareholder in a co-op, you don't own any property. The ownership is in the name of the cooperative, and it pays the overall mortgages and the property taxes.

Nevertheless, you may be able to deduct a proportional share of taxes and mortgage interest, depending on how the corporation is structured. You should get a statement each year from the co-op as to the portion of mortgage interest and taxes you are entitled to deduct. (This is a matter for your accountant or tax specialist to delve into.)

Is a Co-op Purchase a Good Investment?

As with all investments, there are pros and cons. Nevertheless, a good investment is usually determined by how much it increases in value over time. It's fair to ask, therefore, whether a co-op will increase in value as rapidly as a condo or a townhouse.

Unfortunately, there's no pat answer, here. My own observation is that most co-ops, because of their ownership structure, do not increase as rapidly in value as comparable condos or townhouses. The exception, of course, is well-located developments. If you own a co-op in the heart of Manhattan, it's going to be a very valuable asset, one that's likely to see enormous price increases. Indeed, some such co-ops are regularly sold for many millions of dollars.

As with any property purchase, it's a judgment call. Moreover, just because a co-op may be initially inexpensive to get in doesn't make it a good investment. What makes a good home investment is that you're able to enjoy the property while you live there and show a good profit when you sell.

TIP

Take the time to read the co-op prospectus, the balance sheets of the corporation, and the corporate minutes for the past three years. They can tell you much useful information about how the co-op is being run. You may also want to take these documents to an attorney for an opinion.

TIP

Don't know a real estate attorney? Check with your local bar association, which can usually be very helpful. Agents can often make recommendations as well.

10
Should I
Buy New?

Should you buy a brand new condo, townhouse, or co-op from a developer (as opposed to purchasing an existing, "seasoned" unit from an owner)? Are there any advantages to buying new? Any drawbacks?

Most of us like to get things brand new rather than secondhand. We'd prefer a new car to a used one. We'd rather have new clothes than hand-me-downs. The same holds true with where we live.

It's really rather nice to move into a brand-new home, one where no one's used the sinks, tubs, or toilets. The floor covering is new, the walls are all spotless—everything is, presumably, perfect.

On the other hand, buying a new condo, townhouse, or co-op presents certain risks over and above what you'd expect when buying a new single-family house. Let's look at the pros and cons.

What Are the Advantages of Buying Brand New?

It's All New

As we've just discussed, there's nothing quite as nice as a home where no one has lived before. There's such a thing as "new car smell," and there's also such a thing as "new home smell," It's fresh paint, new carpeting, just-laid tile, and so on.

For many people this is a very important plus, not to be diminished. If you really do consider buying brand new a high priority, then by all means do it. My reasoning is simple: If you want brand new and buy existing, you'll never really be happy.

You May Be Able to Upgrade

One of the biggest advantages of buying new is the ability to customize your purchase. While every unit comes with floor covering, it may be inexpensive carpeting that you don't like. However, because it's new the developer will undoubtedly allow you to upgrade (for a price) to a better-quality carpet or a higher-grade tile or wood flooring. This often holds true for countertops, built-in mirrors, appliances, sinks and faucets, and so on.

TIP

In cases where the units haven't yet been built, the builder may be willing to change the layout slightly to suit your needs. You may be able to move a wall a few feet one way or another or add a closet without affecting the overall structure. However, be aware that any changes cost money, sometimes a lot of money, and the builder/developer will expect you to pay it.

You Can Save Money

Sometimes brand-new condo, townhouse, or co-op developments cost less than comparable existing units. One key reason is risk. A new development presents a great many unknowns (discussed among the drawbacks below). You don't know if the development is going to turn out to be a success or end up a failure. You're buying on the hope that everything will come up roses. But it could come up weeds.

Another reason that brand new is less expensive is that very often you're buying direct from the developer—the person or corporation that is putting up the building—without intervening agents. Thus the developer (unlike an existing owner) may not have to pay a real estate commission. Some or all of this saving can be passed on to you.

TRAP

The saving occurs only if the development is selling well. If a development does not sell well, the developer may invite local real estate agents to participate in the sales. Since a commission is now involved, the price of the unit may go up to reflect it.

You Can Make Money

If you buy for a reduced price and your development is successful, you can expect to see an upward price "correction" shortly after it's fully sold out. Typically this occurs within the first three years and is not connected to real estate market conditions.

The reason is that the risk factor, noted above, has been eliminated. Your brand-new home is now an existing unit with a track record—and that's appealing to buyers. As a result, a price bump in a shared ownership development that has aged a year or two is a common phenomenon.

How big a price hike can you hope for? Again, a great deal depends on location, size of units, amenities, and comparables—all the items that go into a valuation. However, some units may jump as much as 30 percent after the first few years. Others may increase as little as 5 percent. And if the development has problems, the price could actually decline!

You Get a Warranty Package

Almost always builders and developers will warrant the construction against defects for a period of time—typically for 10 years. (A warranty is required in some states.) In recent years, however, because of problems builders have had with developments as they approach the 10-year mark, many have begun reducing the time.

The warranty may come directly from the developer or through an insurance company. It is usually comprehensive, covering everything from leaking pipes to broken foundations.

TIP

Be sure to ask if the developer has an emergency number to call if there's a problem. (Just having a warranty package isn't wonderful if you can't get service for six weeks or if you have to sue before the developer honors it.) Call the number. Find out what kinds of service are covered and how quickly someone can get out to help you. Also, find out if you can call a plumber, electrician, or other service to fix an emergency problem and have the warranty pay for it.

What Are the Drawbacks of Buying Brand New?

You Pay More

It may seem like a contradiction to say you pay more for a new unit when I just finished saying you can save money buying new. The truth of the matter is that even though you may initially pay less, for the reasons noted earlier, you could also end up paying more. It depends on the development. The reason has to do with location (inflated land prices) and building costs.

Developers like to put up projects as close to prime real estate residential areas as possible. The reason should be obvious: the new development will benefit from the good reputation of the existing area. This helps ensure that all the units will be in demand and be sold.

However, to develop in an existing high-quality residential area usually means paying top dollar for land. Indeed, most of the land will already be developed, and only a few parcels big enough for a shared ownership development may be left. You can be certain that the owners of these parcels will charge top dollar for them.

Further, the cost of construction—as reflected in the price of both building materials and labor—has gone up considerably over the last decade. Indeed, in some areas, because of the scarcity of available forest land, lumber costs have risen to the point where metal (in the form of studs) is cheaper! As a result of both higher land and construction costs, the developer must charge more for the new shared ownership units than the current price for existing units.

TRAP

Remember that older units may have been put up decades ago when land and building costs were a fraction of what they are today. Even with price increases, the existing units may be far less expensive than brand-new housing, depending on location.

You Don't Know the True Costs for Assessments and Expenses

When you buy brand new, you don't have a track record establishing costs. The developer may tell you that your utilities will run $100 a month and that dues or fees will be another $100. But you can't and shouldn't rely on those figures. The costs could be less, but more than likely will be significantly more.

TRAP

Sometimes, to keep initial assessments or fees low, a developer will not establish an adequate reserve fund or budget sufficient money for maintenance. However, once the units are sold out and the developer no longer participates, the costs could rise, often higher than they would otherwise be to cover deferred maintenance and repairs. The result is that after a few years, your monthly payments could double or more.

TIP

Most states now require shared ownership developers to set aside adequate funds for reserves and maintenance. Check into this with the development you're considering. Be careful to find out if the developer personally is putting in a regular share of money (often a large amount, since the developer represents all unsold units). Sometimes developers will establish reserves, but not fund them.

The Development May Not Be Finished

You take a huge risk if you buy into a new development that is not completed. You could end up losing a great deal. Why would you put money into a development that wasn't finished?

It could look very appealing. Whenever I go out to see a new shared ownership development, I'm struck by the fact that the first things built are the amenities: the swimming pool, spa, sauna, clubhouse, and so on. Typically it's just the amenities and a few models! (This is usually the case with townhouses that are constructed two to four units per building; in a condo development, by contrast, there may be one large building for all units.)

The reason is that the developer wants to show you all the features you can look forward to sharing. You walk in and see that you'll be able to go swimming, play tennis, or whatever, and that's an inducement to buy.

Problems arise when the developer can't finish the project. Sometimes developers are simply poor planners. They thought they could put up the project for a certain amount of money and discover, halfway through, that they can't. So they go bankrupt and the project stalls.

Other times sales just aren't as brisk as anticipated. The developer decides that there's no way the project will sell out in a reasonable amount of time, and abandons it. Or a natural disaster such as a flood or earthquake prevents the developer from getting anticipated financing. For whatever reason, the project folds, only partially finished.

If you purchased one of the early units and the project is terminated before completion, the consequences could be severe. For one thing, dues and fees are predicated on a certain number of units. If only half that number are completed, the costs could be significantly higher.

Further, an unfinished development quickly gets a bad reputation among brokers in the resale market. When a potential buyer asks about it, the agent may say, "Oh, that project went belly up and there are all kinds of lawsuits involving the builder—you don't want to buy there."

Lawsuits involving the builder will complicate any attempt by you to resell. In other words, you could have real trouble getting rid of your unit and may have to sit there for years in a partially completed project.

TIP

It pays to investigate the developer before you buy. What other projects has the builder been involved in? Were they all completed? If so, go out and visit them and see how they're doing. A solid reputation won't guarantee that this project won't go bust, but it's a good start. (Ask the developer for references—*all* previous projects.)

There Could Be Problems With the Building

A few decades ago construction problems with shared ownership developments were a rarity. Today I'm coming to believe that they're the rule. Virtually every brand-new shared ownership development that I've looked into over the past few years has filed a lawsuit against the developer or one of the subcontractors for defects. Sometimes the issues are minor—doors that aren't hung squarely or leaks in plumbing—and can easily be fixed.

Other times, however, the problems are severe—a faulty roof must be replaced or a foundation crumbles to soil slippage—threatening the entire structure. (The soil may not have been sufficiently tested and prepared to handle the structure built on it.)

The problem is due in part to the rush to complete developments and in part to the propensity of owners to file lawsuits at the drop of a hat. Nevertheless, it's an unpleasant problem, one that's all too common in new developments.

TIP

It often takes time for problems to surface. Leaking roofs or bad garage doors may appear within the first year, but ground slippage or foundation cracks take much longer to surface. Many states have a 10-year statute of limitations for taking action against developers; lawsuits can be filed anytime during that decade-long period.

A lawsuit against the developer (or a subcontractor) can drag on for a long time, sometimes years. And the conclusion may or may not be satisfactory. While the owners hope that the developer will be compelled to fix the problem, the result may be that the developer is exonerated—or goes bankrupt.

During the lawsuit, the owners will have to cover attorney's fees and court costs. Plus, they must often pay to have the problem fixed immediately. (You can't live with a leaky roof or a sagging foundation.) Of course, they hope to recoup these costs, but there is no guarantee that will happen.

Further, having a lawsuit on the books inhibits the owners' ability to resell their units. Often lenders won't offer financing on developments involved in lawsuits—particularly if the owners lose and end up being liable for damages. Lenders don't want that kind of risk.

Finally, buyers tend to shy away from developments with lawsuits. Remember, it was one of the warning flags noted in Chapter 4.

What Happens When the Project Sells Out and the Developer Leaves?

If you're considering buying brand new, it's important to understand the role that the developer plays in the project. At the beginning there are no individual owners, only the developer. That means the developer must pay for *all* of the following:

Assessments (dues)

Maintenance costs

Reserve funding

Taxes and insurance

And so on

In other words, everything that the owners will eventually have to pay for collectively the developer must cover individually. On the other hand, the developer has all the votes and can take free rein with the project. The developer can make up, amend, or eliminate rules at will. It's not a democracy, but a totalitarian state.

As Units Sell

As units begin to sell, however, the load on the developer switches to the new owners. With each unit sold the developer has lower costs—for dues and fees, maintenance, reserve funding, and so on—as well as fewer votes.

What typically happens is that the developer becomes sort of a benign dictator, overseeing everything in the development. As long as nothing goes seriously wrong, the new owners are usually content to let things be. Indeed, until the individual buyers amass 51 percent of the total ownership, they may only have limited participation on the board. Rather, control may be held by proxies for the developer.

The problem is that the developer could hold back payments on taxes, money for reserves, and so forth. The project may be in arrears on dues or fees. And because the owners constitute less than half the board, there's little they can do.

After More Than Half the Units Sell

Serious problems often appear after more than half the units are sold. Now the developer is on the home stretch and can see the light at the end of the tunnel. The development will soon be sold out, and it's time to cut costs. However, the new owners want money spent on maintenance, on funding reserves, and on finishing all the units.

TIP

At the tail end of construction, the developer and the owners have different motivations. The developer wants to finish up at the lowest cost and get out. The owners want increased services that will make the development fully operational. As a result, there can be difficult fights between the developer and owners.

As sales dwindle down to the last 10 or 15 units, the developer may refuse to pay proportional dues or fees. The existing homeowners must then come up with the money in order to keep the development fully operational.

TIP

The HOA can record liens on the developer's unsold units preventing it from closing sales until the dues are paid.

At first, the owners may be ineffectual in getting satisfaction from the developer. The reason is that initially the developer ran everything and the owners simply sat back and enjoyed the benefits. Now the owners must elect strong members to the board, obtain a majority, and proceed with things that need be done. All of this is new to them and, as with any first-time effort, leads to mistakes and bickering. As a result, the first board members may have an agenda, but may not know how to accomplish it.

TRAP

 Typically the initial board of directors is filled with cronies of the developer. Since their term of office usually runs from one to three years, it may be quite some time before the owners are able to vote them off the board and get their own representation.

Eventually, the owners get a majority on the board and begin running things their way. A solution is usually arrived at with the developer, who often ends up paying at least a portion of the back dues or fees and reserve funds.

However, things don't always go smoothly. When I joined the board of one development as an owner, it took us four years from the time we got a majority to straighten everything out with the developer. And except for the fact that various board members had exceptional skills in finance, accounting, and management, it could have taken much longer.

Is Buying New a Good Investment?

As we've seen, buying new may or may not prove profitable. There are a lot of risks involved. When you purchase an existing development, one that's at least 10 years old, you pretty much know what you're getting. You can look at a track record of dues and fees, board meetings, even how well the place looks.

But when a development is new, particularly if it's not yet finished, it's a crap shoot. You really don't know whether the devel-

opment will become successful. Even if it does, there's no telling how long it will take.

If you're a risk taker, I would say that you'll probably be happy buying new. But if you prefer to bet only on a sure thing, buying into an existing development may be best for you.

11

What About Buying a Conversion?

Most co-ops and many condominiums are actually conversions. The building started out as an apartment house and later on the owner(s) decided that there was more money to be made by selling the units than by renting them out. So they converted the building. Townhouses, because of their architectural design, normally aren't conversions.

There are some special concerns when buying a conversion that you need to worry about. We covered some of these in Chapter 9, but we'll look into them with more detail here.

Was the Job Cosmetic or Thorough?

It's important to remember that the main motivation of owners who convert buildings to shared ownership developments is financial. They expect to make a profit. And, naturally, the lower the costs of conversion, the more profit there is to be made.

TIP

A cosmetic conversion may cost as little as $10,000 for a 10-unit building. A thorough conversion could cost $100,000 or more for the same 10 units. The question is: Did the owner pay for a full conversion, or will you have to pay more after you buy as problems crop up?

A few years ago, I discussed this very issue with a few property owners in southern California. At the time, converting to condos was big business. These owners stood to make nearly twice as much by selling the building as a condo than by selling it outright as a rental development.

The feeling among the owners was that there was a huge market demand for condo units, yet very few available. Therefore, what they wanted to do was to put a new façade on the building, slap some paint on the rental units, and sell them as condos. In other words, do the least amount of work possible.

I pointed out that the units had some features that were OK for rentals but serious drawbacks for owned units (tiny kitchens, no bathroom off the master bedroom, no laundry facilities). The owners merely scoffed. They countered that it would cost many thousands of dollars per unit to correct those features.

I agreed, but noted that once the work was done, they could sell the units for more, and in the long run the development would be much more successful. I was told in no wasted words that the profit margin would be roughly the same with or without doing the work, so why bother? And since the current owners would be gone as soon as the units sold, why worry about the long term? In short, this was to be a "paint 'em and sell 'em" conversion.

I bowed out of the deal, knowing that buyers of the condo units would be getting an inferior product. The owners went ahead.

TIP

 Owners and developers may be interested in getting units sold with the least cost to them. You should be interested in getting the most for your money.

This is not to say that all conversions are as cosmetic as the example above. Some developers go through the building with a fine-tooth comb and even make structural changes. These are the conversions that stand out, are successful, and over the years tend to appreciate most rapidly in price.

It's just that with any conversion, there's the temptation to do as little as possible, instead of what's truly necessary. The subsequent unit owners are the ones who end up suffering the consequences.

TRAP

A conversion that was only cosmetic or was poorly done may cost you almost as much as one that was done well. But you won't enjoy your tenure of ownership as much. And you could have big problems when it comes time to sell your unit.

Is There a Design Difference Between a Rental Unit and an Owned Apartment?

Rental units are designed for maximum utilization of space. If you have a rental building with 10,000 square feet and you "waste" 3,000 square feet on corridors, balconies, entryways, and so forth, you can rent only seven 1,000-square-foot units. However, if you can reduce that "wasted" area to 1,000 square feet, you can cram two more rental units into the building. The difference between seven units and nine units is 22 percent; that's the increase in rental income you can expect by better utilization of space.

It's important to understand that a rental building owner can get away with such cramming because tenants aren't as particular as owners. Tenants figure they're only going to be renting temporarily. (Almost all tenants truly believe this.) And as a rule, they are willing to put up with much more inconvenience than owners.

TIP

Owners always expect more than tenants. When you buy, you too should expect more from a conversion than if you were looking at a rental. If you don't, when it's time for you to resell, it may be hard to find a buyer with your lower expectations.

How Do I Know If a Resale Unit Was Originally a Conversion?

If you're buying a resale unit from an owner, its history may be difficult to discern. The owner may simply not mention the fact that the building was a conversion. The owner may fail to acknowledge this fact in a disclaimer, although that's certainly something that should be disclosed.

You can find out, however, by checking with the local building and planning departments. They will have on record permits as well as other documents indicating whether the building was put up as a condo or co-op from scratch or was converted from a rental building. You can also tell by some careful examination.

What Do I Look For?

Sometimes it's easy. If the unit you are thinking of buying looks and feels like a room in a motel, chances are it's a conversion. If it looks just like the rental building across the street or next door, chances are it was a conversion. (Often many apartment buildings are put up one next to the other at the same time. Some may have been converted, others not.) Check to see if the layout seems awkward, if there are no washer and dryer facilities, if there's only one bathroom in a unit large enough to need two (1,000 square feet or more), if the kitchen is too tiny—and so on. You get the idea. Sometimes you can just walk through and know immediately that the building was converted, and the job wasn't done very well.

Other times, it's more difficult. The entrance to the building may be spacious, with a large garden area. Hallways are wide. The units have a nice layout, with washing facilities, several bathrooms, and a large and modern kitchen. Is this a conversion or built from the ground up?

Again, you can check with local building and planning departments to be sure. But even so, you may ask, who cares? If it was a conversion, it obviously was done very well. Doesn't that make it just as good as a development built as a condo or co-op from the ground up?

Actually, there are still a number of concerns, which we'll go into shortly. Nevertheless, it is true that a well-done conversion is like a work of art: it can continues to appreciate in value.

How Old Was the Building When It Was Converted?

One of the biggest hidden concerns in a conversion is the true age of the building. And it's a concern whether the job was done well or just cosmetically. Consider: you find a condo being sold by a developer. It's got lots of common areas. The layout and design of the unit are appealing. Everything inside is modern. Indeed, it appears to be brand new. However, when you inquire you discover that it's a conversion. Is there an inherent drawback here?

TRAP

Beware of cosmetic conversions in old buildings. Fresh paint can hide all kinds of structural and system problems that could emerge to haunt you in the years ahead.

Yes, there is. In buying a conversion, you're being asked to pay the value of an essentially new unit. But the building, the basic structure, is old. It could be 10, 20, even 50 years old. So, even though you're getting what appears to be something new, a large part of it is actually much older.

Think of it in terms of cars. Which would you rather have: a brand new Ford or Chevy or a 10-year-old model that's been repainted, had new upholstery installed, and been fitted with new tires?

No matter how much you doll up the used model, it's still an old car. No matter how thorough the conversion, it's still an old building.

What's Wrong With an Old Building?

Although sometimes it may not seem like it, every building has a maximum life span. If it was built poorly, that life span may only be 30 to 50 years. If it was built well, it may be 100 years or more. But eventually the wood will deteriorate, the seams will split, and the building will simply fall down.

Much sooner than this the various systems will fail and need to be repaired or wholly replaced—heating, water, electrical, wiring, waste, elevator, roof, and so forth.

When you buy brand new, assuming the construction is solid, you know that you've got 30 or more years to go in the building. But if you buy a conversion, you may have far less time.

This is the reason that buying a conversion is always a risky business. It's also the reason you need to have a very thorough inspection made of the *entire* premises before you purchase.

What Should an Inspector Look For in Examining a Conversion?

Home inspections are covered separately in Chapter 13. For now, let's consider the job of an inspector who's called in when you know (or suspect) you're going to be buying a conversion.

What you want to know is the age and condition of the following:

1. Foundation

2. Roof

3. Walls, beams, and supports

4. Heating and cooling

5. Electrical and plumbing

6. Sewage disposal

7. Elevator

8. Any other building systems

In a new building all these systems will, presumably, be brand new. In a conversion, unless the owner has replaced everything (most unlikely), some will be in good condition while others will be on their last legs.

If they're in bad shape, you (and the other owners) will have to bear the cost of repair or replacement, sometimes very soon after you purchase. This means that in addition to your purchase price, you may have to dole out many thousands of dollars more.

What About Resale Potential?

If you get the impression that I'm not entirely enthused about conversions, you're right. One of my biggest concerns is resale potential. Even assuming that all the systems, as noted above, are in great shape, there are other factors that *could* contribute to holding the price down when you want to resell.

It Is Really Up to Modern Standards?

There's modern and then there's yesterday-modern. The difference is enormous. Modern means that the latest in fixtures, countertops, cabinets, flooring, ceiling lights, and so on have been installed. There are even modern paint colors and wood stains.

On the other hand, yesterday-modern means what used to be modern a decade or so ago. Instead of Corean or granite countertops, they are laminate. Instead of whitewashed wood cabinets, they are plain brown. Instead of plush carpeting, it's shag. And so on. In other words, when the conversion was made, the developer didn't tear everything out and replace it with new, but instead left many of the older features in place.

TRAP

Watch out if someone tries to sell you on a condo or co-op unit because it's "quaint." This is usually just an attempt to put a better face on an old-fashioned unit.

When walking through a yesterday-modern place, you may feel that some things are a bit old-fashioned, but unless you compare the unit with current-modern it may not seem particularly bad—which is, of course, what the developer is counting on.

However, in 10 years' time what's today-modern will become yesterday-modern. And what's yesterday-modern will become just plain old-fashioned.

In other words, unless you buy today-modern, in 10 years or so your unit will have moved quickly into old-fashioned. And when it comes time to resell (most owners sell within seven to nine years), old-fashioned is not considered desirable.

Does the Layout Make Sense?

One of the big problems with conversions is that the layout was originally designed for a rental. This means that the developer may need to add an extra bathroom or extra closet space, or even combine two rental units into one condo or co-op unit.

Sometimes the conversion works very well and the layout and design of the units are very pleasant. Other times, the results are exceedingly awkward. Not long ago I looked into a building where three units had been converted into two larger units. However, smack dab in the middle of the living room of one of the units was a floor-to-ceiling post.

When I asked the developer why it was there, he pointed out that the post was a necessary part of the structure of the building. It couldn't be removed or replaced by an overhead beam. "But," and he smiled as he said it, "think of it as a conversation piece. You can put hooks on it to hang coats, or add a mirror." Yes, he was trying to make lemonade out of lemons. Still, the solution was exceedingly awkward, a real drawback caused entirely by the conversion. Because of resale problems I wouldn't buy such a unit, and would advise others against it as well.

TIP

 To help determine if the layout makes sense, walk though it once with your eyes open. Then close your eyes and try to visualize the floor plan. If it's easy to do, chances are the layout works. If you can't remember what room leads where, there could be a design problem.

If there's a post in the living room or a bedroom next to the kitchen, or you enter via a narrow hallway, or the dining room is across the living room instead of next to the kitchen, you've got an awkward design, probably made necessary by the conversion. My suggestion is that if you think it's awkward, so will potential buyers when it comes time to resell. Better to look for units with an attractive design and layout.

Are All Appliances Available?

Tenants don't mind going out of their units to a central laundry room to wash and dry their clothes. Owners do. If you're asked to buy a unit that doesn't have a clothes washer and dryer area (with necessary electrical, water, gas, and wastewater disposal hookups), my suggestion is you pass on it. You'll hate it every time you need to lug the clothes down to the laundry area and back. Future buyers will not look favorably on it either.

The same goes for other appliances. The kitchen should have a dishwasher and a garbage disposal. There should be room for a large refrigerator. (Even if yours is small, the next buyer's may be large.) There should be sufficient counter space for preparing meals as well as for accommodating small appliances like a toaster, microwave, and coffee maker.

Remember, you can talk yourself into believing that you can live with less than adequate. But will you be able to talk the next buyer into it when you want to resell?

Are the Bathroom Fixtures Modern?

Modern toilets have low-flow tanks to reduce water usage. They also come in a variety of colors and can have striking designs. If you're not sure how old the toilet is in the unit you're considering, lift the tank top off and turn it over. The date it was manufactured will likely be stamped there—and that's usually pretty close to the date it was installed.

TRAP

 Beware of new sinks and faucets connected to old plumbing. Turn on the tap. Does the water run freely with good flow? Does it go down the drain quickly? If not, there could be a problem.

What about the bathroom sink(s)? A modern sink and faucet are in order. Is there a shower or tub with a glass door? (A shower curtain is definitely old-fashioned, although in some bathrooms with antique tubs, it's now becoming fashionable.) If so, check the metal around the door. It should be smooth with no discoloration. The metal used for shower doors is usually plated with chrome, gold, or antique-colored alloys. Over time and with exposure to heat and water, the plated layer breaks down, discolors, and even peels. A modern bathroom will not have discolored or peeling metal fixtures.

The bathroom floors should be of good material, typically tile of some sort, although wood or even carpeting can be found in some "modern" bathrooms. The bathroom walls should be covered with a gloss paint that can easily be washed.

You may not consider these important items, until it comes time to resell and you find potential buyers complaining about them.

What's the Bottom Line?

If the inspection reveals no problems, if the building wasn't very old when converted, if the conversion was thorough and the units are now truly modernized, you should do very well with the purchase. A well-done conversion is just as good as a condo or co-op built that way from the ground up. Indeed, because a conversion may have the added benefit of being in a close-in urban location, it may even be better.

On the other hand, the inspection may reveal that only cosmetic work was done. If heating, plumbing, or other systems were not replaced, if the unit has a poor layout or isn't modern, if required appliances and features are lacking, then I suggest you reconsider. You probably won't enjoy the unit as much as one that was built from the ground up. And reselling later on could be a problem.

12

Converting Your Condo, Townhouse, or Co-op to a Rental

Although most of us don't anticipate renting out our condo, townhouse, or co-op when we buy it, there may come a time when renting is a necessity. We may find we need to move elsewhere and can't sell the unit, so we want to rent it out to help meet the payments. Or perhaps some calamity has befallen us, such as illness or loss of employment, and we must rent out in order to preserve our credit or even keep the unit out of foreclosure. Or perhaps we one day decide we want a real estate investment and feel the best course is to convert our condo to a rental. Finally, maybe we are "owner investors" from the start: we bought initially with the goal of renting.

Whatever the reason, renting out a condo, townhouse, or co-op presents problems different from renting other types of residential real estate. There are usually restrictions as well as extra responsibilities. And there are the overall problems any landlord faces with property. We'll look into all these concerns here.

TRAP

Condos do not generally make good rentals. Often when you add up the costs for mortgage, taxes, insurance, assessments, maintenance, and any other fees you as a landlord will pay, the expenses far exceed the rental income. In other words, condos are often "alligators"; they chew up your money. You might be better off selling the unit than trying to rent it.

Are There Restrictions Against Renting?

Generally speaking, if you own property one of the rights you get with it (in addition to the right to sell it) is the right to rent or lease it. This is usually inviolate. However, if the development was built with government subsidies for lower-income housing, the CC&Rs can prohibit rerenting.

TRAP

Remember, with a co-op you don't directly own any real estate; you own stock in a corporation that owns the real estate. And you have a lease on a unit in the development. Your co-op lease and/or the rules of the co-op may specifically prohibit the renting out of your unit. You should check building policy carefully before purchasing.

Many times there are rental restrictions which take many forms. Some condo or townhouse developments have none at all. Others, particularly co-ops, have rather strict rules. All the restrictions, however, are normally contained in the CC&Rs, bylaws, and rules passed by the board. These should be readily available to you, so you can learn what they are before you purchase or convert. Here are some typical restrictions.

Number of Occupants. You may be limited in the number of people who can occupy your unit. This is usually to limit the density of the development so that there aren't too many people using the swimming pool or tennis courts. For example, you may be restricted to no more than four people per unit.

TRAP

Federal antidiscrimination laws prohibit discriminating against families with children when renting. That means that if a family with five children wants to rent your unit, you may not be able to turn these renters down unless your unit is too small to accommodate them. A real problem occurs when the rules of the development conflict with federal guidelines. Your condo HOA may tell you that you can rent only to four people while the federal government insists that you rent to more.

Number of Cars or Motorcycles. You may be limited to tenants with only one or two cars per unit and motorcycles below a certain maximum noise level.

Where Signs Can Be Placed. One of the ways you find tenants is to put a big "For Rent" sign on your property. However, the development may prohibit putting up such signs anywhere on the common areas, which may include areas outside your unit.

TIP

Some landlords get past sign restrictions by putting up a "For Rent" notice within a window of the unit. While your board probably can't prohibit signs, it can establish guidelines for their use.

Use of Recreational Facilities by Tenants. The HOA may try to prohibit tenants from using the swimming pool, spa, tennis court, golf course, or other recreational facilities. The rationale is usually to limit usage when such facilities are overcrowded (not really big enough to accommodate even the owners). Studies have found that tenant usage of recreational facilities tends to be far higher than owner usage!

TIP

It's not clear that an HOA can restrict you from transferring your use of recreational facilities to a tenant, provided your dues are not in arrears and there are no other charges against you. If the usage runs with your title, you may have an excellent case. The problem, of course, is that the HOA or board may not agree and may go ahead and enforce such restrictions. Your ultimate recourse may be to get an attorney and fight the HOA. As always in such matters, the outcome is never guaranteed. (A better solution, in the long term, is to replace the board with members more favorable to your cause.)

Other Restrictions.   It's important to remember that the rules of the development are created by owners elected to the board. The variety, complexity, and downright orneriness of those rules are limited only by the board's imagination. Before attempting to rent out your unit, check with the board to see what, if any, arcane restrictions against renting have been instituted.

TIP

You may have some control over renting based on state laws and prior legal cases. Check with an attorney.

TRAP

A restriction against renting may come from an unexpected source: your mortgage lender. Most buyers specifically state on the loan application that they intend to use the property as their personal residence.

In such cases, very often their mortgage will contain a clause to the effect that vacating the premises and renting it out is cause for calling in the mortgage (foreclosing). While the chances of the lender actually foreclosing are remote (I have heard of it happening but have never witnessed it myself), it is something to think about.

What Are Your Responsibilities to the Development?

On the other side of the coin, you have certain responsibilities to other owners when you rent out your shared ownership unit. While these may not be evident initially, they may come into play during the tenancy.

Tenant Must Abide by Rules.   Just as you as an owner must abide by the bylaws and rules of the shared ownership development, so must your tenant. For example, there may be prohibitions against loud parties after 10 p.m., parking a car in the driveway (as opposed to in the garage), keeping dogs in the unit, or exceeding a speed limit of, say, 10 mph within the complex. Your tenant must avoid parties, driveway parking, dogs, and speeding.

The problem, however, is that the HOA doesn't have any direct control over renters. Your tenant isn't the owner of the unit; you are. Therefore, if the tenant breaks the rules, the HOA will notify you, censure you, fine you, and possibly take other actions. You'll then have to take action yourself against the tenant.

Therefore, it is incumbent upon you to give your tenant a complete list of the rules of the development. Make it clear (both verbally and in writing in the lease or rental agreement) that you expect the tenant to obey them, and put in penalties if the tenant fails to comply. In short, just as the HOA will come down on you if the tenant breaks the rules, you must be prepared to come down on the tenant.

Tenant Must Maintain the Premises.   There may be some external areas that owners are required to maintain. If so, then your tenant must maintain these areas just as you would. An alternative for many owners is to hire a gardener or caretaker to make sure that these areas are kept in good shape during the tenancy. (It's usually a mistake to count on the tenant to do the work.)

Tenant Must Meet Approval of Other Owners.   Approval is not an issue with a condo development. But it may be the case with a co-op that allows you to sublet or lease your unit. Just as the board may want to approve any buyer you sell to, so it may want to approve any tenant you rent to—assuming the board allows you to rent out your unit at all. The tenant may need to meet strict financial and other criteria.

TIP

When renting, be sure that your tenant fully understands that the unit is part of a shared ownership development. Some tenants simply don't know there's a difference and think that a condo or townhouse is just cheaper to rent than a single-family detached home. (It often is.) You'll avoid lots of problems if early on you make it very clear to the tenant that there's a difference and what that difference is.

Do I Need a Lease?

Of course you do, or at least a tenancy agreement. When you rent out your unit, you become a landlord. And as a landlord you need to protect your investment. A lease is one important part of doing that. As the landlord of a condo, townhouse, or co-op unit, you also will need to do all of the following:

1. Advertise and find tenants.
2. Do a credit check on tenants (with prospective tenant's permission).
3. Call previous landlords to see if prospective renters were good tenants (with prospective tenant's permission).
4. Show the unit.
5. Have the chosen tenants sign a lease or tenancy agreement.
6. Get security, breakage, pet, and other deposits.

7. Do a walk-through before the move-in to let tenants know there is no damage or, if there is, to identify it.

8. Collect rent.

9. Talk to tenants who are late with rent.

10. Evict tenants who fail to pay rent or break the lease.

11. Do a walk-through with tenants before they leave to be sure they haven't done any damage.

12. Return appropriate amounts of deposits.

13. Rerent.

TIP

Being a landlord is both art and science, and doing it right takes patience, intelligence, and good luck. There are several good books on the market, such as *The Landlord's Troubleshooter* and *the Landlord's Handbook,* that can help you in your endeavors as a landlord (as well as provide lease forms).

TIP

There are all sorts of local, state, and federal guidelines that you must follow as a landlord. Don't simply think you can jump in and do as you want. For example, if your property was built prior to 1978, you *must* provide tenants with a statement (before they move in) of whether, to your knowledge, the unit contains lead-based paint. You must also provide them with a booklet on lead-based paint. Learn the rules and don't get in trouble as a landlord.

How Much Should I Charge for Rent?

Your maximum rental rate will be determined by the rental market. You won't be able to charge more than other landlords are charging

for similar units. Therefore, the first thing you need to do is to find
out the going rates.

The place to start is in your own development. If you're renting,
chances are so are others. In many developments 10 percent or
more of the units are rented out. Go to the HOA or board and see
if it has a list of tenant-occupied units along with a list of owners of
the units. (Many HOAs and boards keep such lists.) Then call some
of the owners and ask about their rental experience.

While a few may be uncooperative, most owners will be happy to
tell you what their relationship has been (good or bad) with the
HOA or board and with tenants, and how much they've been able
to charge for rent. You may discover very quickly that the ceiling for
units just like yours is $750 a month, or $1500 a month, or $350 a
month, or whatever. Now you know what to rent your unit for.

TRAP

Don't think that because your unit is better decorated,
more modern, or even better located within the development, you'll be able to command a much higher
rent. You may get a few bucks more, but tenants are
pretty sophisticated these days and they usually know
what a given unit in a given development should rent
for. (They learn the ropes very quickly as they look for
rentals.) They won't pay you more than your neighbor
will charge them to rent a similar unit.

If for some reason you can't find out what other units in your
development are renting for, or if there aren't other units for rent,
then check out the overall rental market. Take a weekend, prefer-
ably at the end of the month (when most rental ads come out), to
check out advertised units that seem similar to yours. Go to see them
as a pretend would-be tenant, and find out what the rents are. You'll
very quickly learn what the market is for rentals and discover how
much you can charge.

By the way, also find out how most other landlords are handling
utilities, dues or fees, and other charges. In some cases the landlord
pays these out of the rent. In other cases the tenant pays them on
top of the rent.

Should I Become a Landlord?

You may not have a choice about becoming landlord. Circumstance may force you to rent out your unit in order to keep financially afloat. On the other hand, you may simply be toying with the idea as an investment.

My advice is that you consider it very carefully. I've been a landlord for more than 20 years and have done it quite successfully. Yet I would clearly say that it is not for everyone.

As a landlord, you become a servant to your property. That means if the tenant has a problem—a leaky faucet, a disagreement with a neighbor, or a broken garage door opener—you're the one who must solve it. You'll get calls at work, at dinner, on the weekends, and in the middle of the night. Some problems must be taken care of immediately.

TIP

One solution is to hire a property management firm. However, this can be an expensive answer. Most PM firms charge 10 percent of your rental income or more for management. And all repair and maintenance costs are billed separately on top of that, often at the professional rate for plumbers, electricians, and so on. (Some firms do offer reduced rates for repairpeople they work with regularly.)

TRAP

Never try to rent property that's more than an hour's distance away from your home. Long-distance landlording can be *very* expensive, time-consuming, and ineffective. It's a personal job and you'll find yourself trying to solve problems over the phone, hiring plumbers or electricians long distance and having to accept their evaluations and costs, or driving/flying back and forth to the rental to solve problems. Yes, you can rent long distance and I've done it. But in most cases, it simply isn't worth the hassle.

Can I Write Off My Rental Costs?

Maybe, maybe not. The IRS has tightened its rules about writing off losses from rental property against personal income. Generally speaking, you can't take a write-off if your income exceeds $150,000; there are sliding-scale rules for lower incomes. Further, you must actively participate in the management of the unit, and there are other limitations. Be sure to check with your accountant here.

13

Checking the Disclosures and Having an Inspection

Today when you buy any home, whether it is a single-family detached dwelling or a condo, townhouse, or co-op, there are two things that you should get prior to concluding the sale: disclosure of defects (if any) from the seller and an inspection.

What Are Disclosures?

In the old days sellers would conceal defects in the homes they were selling. They would paint over cracks in the walls, fail to mention a leaky roof or a broken foundation, and generally "let the buyer beware."

Not so today. Currently at least 22 states require sellers to disclose to buyers any defects they know of (or should know of) in the property. Disclosures are commonly given to buyers by sellers in the remainder of states as well.

Smart sellers *want* you to know if there are any defects in the home they are selling. The reason is simple. If you know about the defect and buy the property anyway, it's much harder for you to come back later on and complain (and demand that the seller fix the problem or compensate you).

Not all sellers are smart. Many today still try to conceal defects, which is another reason you want your own inspection.

Can I Rely on Disclosures?

Yes, and no. You can rely on disclosures if they reveal something. If a seller reveals that there's water in the basement in winter, you can be sure the water will be there. On the other hand, you can't rely on all sellers revealing all defects. Some they may try to conceal; others they may simply not know about.

Generally speaking, you can tell if the seller is smart about disclosures by the number of them. A savvy seller will attempt to disclose everything. The list may be dozens of items long. While something important could still be left off, a long list does suggest that the seller is serious about letting you know of possible defects.

On the other hand, I'd worry about a seller who presented me with a sheet of paper that blithely said, "No defects." All homes have *some* defects—even if it's nothing more than a broken window screen or a fence that's leaning over.

What Should I Do With the Disclosures?

There are three steps to dealing with disclosures. We'll look at each in turn.

1. Make Approval of the Disclosures a Contingency of Purchase.
Learning that the property has defects will do you no good unless you can then take some action. In some states you can back out of the deal without penalty within a certain number of days after receiving the disclosures. In California, for example, you have three days to approve them. If you don't approve them, there's no deal. Other states have different time limits. Check with an agent about the rules for disclosure in your state.

If your state doesn't have specific rules, you can make the sale contingent upon your approval of the disclosures. For example, you can write a clause into the purchase agreement stating that you have X number of days to approve the seller's disclosures. If you don't approve them, there is no purchase. (Have an attorney or a knowledgeable agent write in the exact words for you.)

Making the deal contingent on your approval of the disclosures is critical to protecting you. For example, what if a seller discloses that the townhouse you want to buy is actually on a landslide and is slowly slipping down the hill? If it were me, I'd seriously consider backing out of that deal!

More than likely, of course, there will be nothing seriously wrong with the property and the seller's disclosures will reveal very little. In that case, you'll want to move forward.

2. Check Over the Disclosures Carefully. Resist the temptation simply to toss the disclosures into a pile with other documents involved in the purchase. (By the time you finish buying the property, you'll probably have a folder several inches thick with documents ranging from the purchase agreement to loan forms.)

That's a mistake. You want to scrutinize the disclosures. Most important, you want to try to read between the lines. Wily sellers may try to disclose things in a way that makes something serious appear to be something minor. Let's look briefly at some real-life examples:

- "Uneven foundation." Translated, the foundation is severely cracked and pieces of it are splayed out at different angles.

- "Minor color variations in the ceiling." Translated, the roof leaks so badly that water has run down and discolored the ceiling.

- "Attractive water courses on side of house." Translated, rainwater washes down the hillside in winter and runs in a river on both sides of the home.

Take everything the seller writes down seriously. Ask questions to be sure you thoroughly understand what is being described. Ask for written clarifications. Something that seems to be innocuous could actually be just the start of a buyer's nightmare.

3. Renegotiate Purchase on the Basis of the Disclosures.   If you find something seriously wrong, consider either backing out of the deal or renegotiating it. Keep in mind that in the vast majority of cases, defects can be cured with enough money.

TRAP

Not all defects are curable. Some broken foundations, land slippage, and water problems cost so much to fix (if a fix is even possible) that the house simply isn't worth it at any price.

If you decide that you want to renegotiate the price, let the seller know that you disapprove the disclosures. However, you would be willing to accept them *if* the owner, for example:

- Repairs or replaces the existing roof.
- Patches and repaints the cracks inside and out.
- Puts in a sump pump to control basement flooding.
- Replaces leaking galvanized pipes with new copper plumbing.
- Gives you credit for a certain amount of cash in escrow to cover the cost of repairs.
- Does whatever else is necessary to make you feel comfortable going forward with the deal.

Will the seller comply with your demand(s)? Usually a seller will, or at least will counteroffer. Let's say it costs $10,000 to put on a new roof. The seller may agree to pay half or two-thirds, or may credit you with $4000 toward your nonrecurring (one-time) closing costs in escrow. Now, it's a matter of going back and forth to see if a compromise can be worked out that both you and the seller will accept.

TIP

Keep in mind that the seller wants to dump the home. If you come back with demands after disclosures, chances are other buyers will as well. It's to the seller's advantage to deal with you (since you're already involved in the purchase) rather than turn you down and hope another buyer comes along who will make fewer (or no) demands.

TRAP

Not all sellers do what is in their own best interests. Even though it may make perfectly good sense to compromise, a seller may simply refuse and demand that you take the home "as is." Your options are to do so, at your peril, or walk away and find another condo, townhouse, or co-op with a more cooperative seller.

Why Do I Need an Inspection?

You need to know what you're buying. If a condo in perfect condition is worth $100,000, what's a condo with a broken furnace or a cracked slab worth? I can guarantee it's worth something less. You don't want to pay full price for a product that, because of a problem, is worth less.

Further, you want the condo, townhouse, or co-op to be in good condition when you move in. The last thing you need is to get the property in October only to find that the furnace is out and it will cost you $2000 to keep warm over the next winter. Or that the air conditioning doesn't work and you'll need to spend $1500 to keep cool next summer.

TRAP

Occasionally sellers produce an inspection report they have already obtained and paid for. They may insist that you go with their report and not order your own. Don't honor their demands. You don't know who the inspector was (the seller's cousin?) or how thorough an inspection was done. Perhaps most important, you don't have the oral comments of the inspector. Remember, you're paying for the inspection and you should be entitled to it. Treat any seller who refuses to let you conduct your own inspection as potentially hiding a serious defect in the property.

Finally, the inspection could reveal something so serious that you'd want to reconsider your purchase. If there is something truly wrong with the property, you want to learn of it before you purchase, not after!

What If It's a Conversion?

A condo or co-op conversion presents special problems. Although conversions are covered in detail in Chapter 11, some points bear repeating. You will want to be reassured of the following:

- The conversion was done properly, following accepted construction practices.
- All the building's systems (plumbing, electrical, heating, wastewater, and so on) are in good shape and will not soon need repair or replacement.
- The structure (particularly an older building) is sound.
- There are no defects in other parts of the building (major leaks, slippage, cracks, and so on) that could affect your unit at a later date.

TIP

Be sure to check local building department records to see that the developer took out appropriate permits for the conversion. These days just about everything from moving walls to exchanging a dishwasher requires a permit. Work done without a permit might have to be redone with a permit at a later date.

What Will It Cost?

The typical cost of a home inspection these days is between $200 and $350. However, if you want to get a thorough inspection of a condo, townhouse, or co-op—including the overall structure—it could cost more.

It normally takes an hour or two to inspect an individual unit. Add a couple of more hours for the basement, attic, and so on of the overall structure and even more time for a detailed inspection of various systems such the elevator, heating and cooling, and plumbing.

TRAP

Occasionally a board will not want you to inspect anything other than the unit you are purchasing. The usual explanation is that a more thorough inspection inconveniences other owners. (This is normally not true of inspecting the basement or roof, but it may be true of inspecting electrical wiring or plumbing.) It's hard for you, as a purchaser, to insist, although the seller may be able to implore the board to allow the inspection. If the board still refuses, you may have to decide whether to purchase without a thorough inspection.

Where Do I Find an Inspector?

Inspectors are plentiful these days. Just check the phone book under "Home Inspection" and you should find many. However, it's better to get an inspector by referral. Often agents can recommend inspectors, as can friends or relatives who have recently purchased a home.

However you come up with an inspector, be sure to interview the person carefully. To my knowledge, few states have yet instituted licensing or regulation of home inspectors. Therefore, it's up to you to separate the good from the bad.

My suggestion is that you interview some candidates and then ask them for references—people whose homes they have previously inspected. Then call the owners and find out their impression. Did the inspector do a thorough job or was the work superficial? Did they later discover anything that the inspector should have noticed?

Finally, check the inspector's qualifications. My own preference is for someone with a professional degree (such as structural engineering) or someone who was previously a building inspector for a city or county. Be cautious if someone was simply a contractor. This person may or may not have the breadth of experience necessary to conduct a thorough inspection.

TIP

Check that the inspector belongs to a trade organization such as ASHI (American Society of Home Inspectors) or NAHI (National Association of Home Inspectors).

What Do I Do If the Inspection Reveals Serious Problems?

You hope that the inspection will be thorough and will reveal nothing bad about the property. Unfortunately, that's not always the case. Sometimes defects are uncovered. What do you do now?

You follow the three rules discussed earlier with regard to disclosures.

1. Make Approval of the Inspection a Contingency of Purchase. You can and should make the purchase contingent upon your approval of the inspection. Write into the purchase agreement that you have a period of time (typically two weeks) to inspect the property. Further, make the purchase contingent upon your approving the inspection report.

TIP

Sellers these days readily accept an inspection approval contingency. They just assume that no savvy buyer would purchase a home without one. If sellers refuse, they could be hiding a serious defect.

Making the deal contingent on your approval of the inspection report is critical to protecting you. Without the contingency, what would you do if you found something seriously wrong? You'd still be obliged to continue with the purchase!

2. Check Over the Report Carefully. As with disclosures, the devil is in the details. Look for small things that could suggest something bigger. Discovery of mold growing on the wall of a bathroom, in itself of little consequence, could suggest a serious leak in the plumbing. Water stains on the ceiling rafters are of no consequence except that they suggest the roof is leaking.

TIP

Go with the inspector. You will learn far more from the inspector's oral comments than from anything that gets written in the report. Too often inspectors are hesitant to commit their educated opinion to writing. But most will be happy to tell you that they think the place is falling down and you'd be a fool to buy it.

Be aware that inspectors always put in a host of disclaimers. Be prepared for many paragraphs warning you that the report does not cover anything the inspector could not visually see (such as floors covered by carpeting) and so on. These days inspectors try to cover themselves as much as possible against lawsuits by angry purchasers who discovered that a serious defect was overlooked in an inspection.

3. Renegotiate Purchase on the Basis of the Inspection. If you find something seriously wrong, consider either backing out of the deal or renegotiating it. I know buyers who have had the price of property reduced 30 percent or more on the basis of a bad inspection report.

Remember, once the report is in, a savvy seller will have to give it to all future buyers. (Otherwise, those future buyers may come back and claim the seller did not make full disclosure.) That means the seller is on the spot. The seller can either resolve the problem with you or settle it with some future buyer. Since you're already there, why not deal with you?

It now comes down to a matter of negotiation. Will the seller fix the problem or give you a credit in escrow of a certain amount of cash? Can the problem be easily remedied? Will you accept the problem if it's endemic to the building—for a reduced price? The better a negotiator you are, the more you'll get out of a bad inspection report.

TIP

Some buyers hope for a bad inspection report. Indeed, they look for properties where a bad report is likely. Their goal is to use it as leverage to renegotiate a much lower price.

Will a Home Warranty Plan Protect Me?

Sellers will often pay for a home warranty protection plan. These plans provide that if certain problems occur in the home, the insurance company (rather than the seller) will automatically cover them.

The warranty plan usually covers such items as:

- Plumbing, including dishwasher and garbage disposal
- Electrical, including built-in appliances
- Heating and cooling systems

For an extra premium, the plan may also cover:

- Pool or spa pump and motor
- Roof leaks
- Other, more serious defects

It's important to understand, however, that the warranty plan requires the seller to sign a statement acknowledging that, as of the close of escrow, the property is in good condition with no defects. If there are known defects, the warranty plan will usually exclude them from coverage.

Hence, while the warranty plan is very useful for covering small problems that may later turn up (such as a leaking water heater or a broken furnace), it provides little or no protection against more serious defects, particularly those disclosed or discovered prior to the close of sale.

Check into Chapter 15 for additional clues on handling inspection reports.

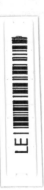

14

Where to Get Financing

I'm quite confident that all of us would like nothing more than to purchase our next home for cash. However, in the real world that's seldom the case. (Actually, according to statistics well over 15 percent of home purchases are, indeed, for cash!)

Like most of us, you'll need to finance your purchase. The question now becomes: Where do you get financing for your condo, townhouse, or co-op purchase? We'll get the answers in this chapter.

What Are My Financing Sources?

The following lenders offer mortgages on condos and townhouses and some of them on co-ops:

Banks

Builders and developers

Credit unions

Mortgage bankers

Mortgage brokers

Online lenders

Savings and loans

Sellers

Let's consider each one separately.

TIP

No matter which lender you use, it is required to give you a good-faith estimate of your costs at the time you apply for the mortgage. This is part of RESPA (Real Estate Settlement Procedures Act). This allows you to see what the mortgage is going to cost you up front and to shop around for a lower-cost loan. Most lenders comply with RESPA; however, enforcement has been less than strict. As a consequence, you should be aware that some lenders will "accidentally" leave out costs which then appear only as you're ready to close the deal. Your best bet for avoiding this is to ask a good mortgage broker or agent to point you toward a reputable lender.

Can I Get a Bank Loan?

Probably, if you want it. Your commercial banker may be willing to help finance your shared ownership purchase. However, banks are not known for their low interest rates or their favorable terms on their "keeper" loans—ones they make from their own reserves and hold. Other sources may be better. (See portfolio loans, below.)

However, most banks should be able to get you a "conforming" loan. This is a mortgage underwritten by one of the nation's two largest quasi-public secondary lenders: Fannie Mae or Freddie Mac. The bank loans you the money, then sells your mortgage to the secondary market. To qualify you must have superior credit, a good history of employment (the ability to repay), and strong reserves (extra cash in the bank). However, a large down payment is not required. Conforming loans are available for down payments of 20 percent, 10 percent, 5 percent, or even less. And conforming loans typically offer the lowest interest rates.

TIP

When comparing interest rates, keep in mind that the true yield of the loan—the amount you actually pay for it—includes the interest rate, the points, and the fees

(which can be high). Thus a mortgage with a low interest rate and lots of points and fees can end up costing
you more than a mortgage with a higher interest rate
but no points and fewer fees. Check the end of this
chapter for a description of how points and the interest rate interact.

A bank may also be willing to offer you a "portfolio" loan. This is
a mortgage held in the bank's own portfolio rather than sold to a
secondary lender. Typically these are for amounts over the maximum for conforming loans (currently $240,000). As stated earlier,
they carry a higher interest rate.

Some banks may be willing to offer loans on stock pledges for
those who want to buy co-ops. Call to find out if your bank makes this
type of financing. Finally, banks are used to making personal loans.
If for some reason you can't get financing on the property, you may
be able to, in effect, get financing on yourself. Be sure to ask.

Will Builders or Developers Offer Me Financing?

If you're buying new (or a new conversion), be sure to find out
whether financing is available through the builder or developer's
lender. It goes without saying that in order to sell large numbers of
condos, townhouses, or co-ops, the developer or builder will almost
certainly need to come up with financing.

This source of financing may not offer the lowest interest rate or
the most favorable terms, but it may be the easiest to get (perhaps
the only outlet available to you). Further, in some cases the builder
or developer may "buy down" the loan as a further enticement to
make a purchase.

TIP

A "buy-down" means that the builder or developer will
pay the lender an extra sum of money so that you can
get a lower interest rate. Sometimes the lower rate will
apply for just the first few years of the mortgage. (For

example, for the first three years the loan would be at 6 percent, then jump up to 7 percent for the remainder of the term.) In other cases the lower rate may apply for the entire term. Be sure to ask about any buydown features as well.

Can I Get a Credit Union Loan?

You must belong to a credit union to use its financing. Currently membership in most credit unions is expanding. Check to see if any groups you belong to (your employer, club, or other organization) also have a credit union.

Credit unions often make conforming loans like banks; they also offer a wide variety of other financing. Their interest rates and points are not usually lower than market. Where you can save a lot of money, however, is in the fees. Most credit unions do not charge large fees, particularly so-called garbage fees tacked on by other lenders.

TRAP

Garbage fees are arbitrary costs that the lender adds in when you get the mortgage. They are usually added for the purpose of increasing the lender's yield on the loan. In other words, they effectively increase your interest rate over the life of the loan. (A 6 percent loan with $2000 in fees may end up being a 7 percent loan!) Avoid garbage fees whenever possible.

What Is a Mortgage Banker?

A mortgage banker is a bank that specializes in real estate financing. Unlike a commercial bank, the mortgage bank does not offer checking or savings accounts, personal loans, or other types of consumer services. It offers *only* mortgages. For this reason, it is an excellent source of financing.

Mortgage bankers that deal directly with consumers (not all do) advertise as such in the phone book, on television and radio, and over the Internet. They typically offer conforming loans plus a small variety of other types. Their rates are very competitive.

Should I Use a Mortgage Broker?

Just as a real estate agent "peddles" real estate, a mortgage broker peddles mortgages. A good mortgage broker will have dozens, perhaps hundreds of sources—including banks, mortgage bankers, savings and loans, credit unions, and insurance companies (which do not normally make direct loans to consumers). Because of the large number of financing sources, the mortgage broker can usually offer you the greatest variety of loans and the best service.

TIP

You shouldn't have to pay the mortgage broker a fee to get a loan. Rather, the fees are paid by the lender. Further, the cost of the mortgage shouldn't be any higher than going to the lender directly. The reason is that the mortgage broker is a retailer, while the lender is a wholesaler. No matter where you as a consumer go, you'll end up paying retail. (The one exception may be borrowing online, as discussed below.)

Mortgage brokers can usually offer you conforming or portfolio loans as well as other types (asset-based, equity-financed, and so on). When looking for financing, check here first.

What About Borrowing on the Internet?

The Internet is the fastest-growing source of real estate financing. It is still, however, in its infancy, generating less than 5 percent of all mortgages.

However, borrowing online offers some amazing advantages, including discounts. The discounts are possible because the lender doesn't have to pay the overhead costs of a storefront, sales force, and so on. Some of these savings can be passed on to you. Typically, the interest rates and points of online lenders are lower than those of storefront lenders, whether they be brokers, banks, or other sources.

Online lenders include mortgage brokers as well as direct lenders such as banks and mortgage bankers. Here are some of my favorites:

http://www.eloan.com   In my opinion, this is one of the best mortgage lenders on the Internet, offering low rates plus complete descriptions of loan terms including any garbage fees.

http://www.homeshark.com   This independent has an excellent Web site and many different loan programs, some with discounts.

http://www.homefair.com   Home Fair is an independent mortgage lender site offering a wide variety of mortgage financing.

http://www.mortgage.quicken.com   QuickenMortgage comes from Intuit, the people who gave us the Quicken home financial programs. Its wizard/calculator is one of the best I've found. As of this writing, the site offers mortgages from six national lenders.

http://www.hud.gov   HUD (the federal government's Department of Housing and Urban Development) does not offer mortgages online, but it has an incredible wealth of mortgage-hunting information that should prove invaluable.

http://www.fanniemae.com   Fannie Mae is the country's largest secondary lender. You won't find many consumer mortgage loans here, but you will find all sorts of information on mortgages. (Much of it, unfortunately, is highly technical.) This is a good resource for the more advanced mortgage hunter.

http://www.freddiemac.com   Freddie Mac is the nation's second-largest secondary lender. Again no loans are made directly to consumers, but the site is filled with helpful tips. Information tends to be less technical and more consumer-oriented than Fannie Mae's.

Should I Try a Savings and Loan?

Go ahead, if you can still find one. After the debacle of the late 1980s, when so many S&Ls went under (along with the federal insurance agency that guaranteed them), most S&Ls converted to mutual savings banks.

Savings and loans were the traditional lenders for real estate. They often had large portfolios of loans and were the most versatile in making loans that were personalized—created to suit each borrower's individual needs.

Don't Forget Sellers

Just as the developer or builder of a new property must offer financing to get new units sold, so sellers of existing condos, townhouses, and co-ops often offer financing to help make the sale. Financing typically takes the form of a second mortgage on a condo or townhouse or a collateralized loan on a co-op.

Don't overlook seller financing. Frequently it's the best you can get. In order to make a sale, the seller may be willing to offer you a lower-than-market interest rate. Further, sellers normally do not charge points or fees.

TIP

 You may get the seller to just charge interest, instead of interest plus principal, which will get you a lower payment. Also, the seller will often make only the most cursory check of your credit, perhaps just a local credit report, and may not care about your income or other resources. This means that you may be able to get seller financing where you otherwise would not qualify for institutional financing.

TRAP

With seller financing, the terms of the loan are created by agreement between you and the seller. This means the seller could put in all sorts of onerous terms. You want to be sure that terms for payback are reasonable. Pay special attention to any balloon payments which require you pay back the entire loan by a certain date, long before it fully amortizes (pays off in equal monthly payments). There's nothing wrong with this, provided you understand it's there and can refinance or sell the property at the time the balloon is due.

What Special Features of Real Estate Financing Should I Be Aware Of?

There are many. Here are a few key features.

What Are Points?

A point represents 1 percent of the mortgage amount. One point of a $100,000 mortgage is $1000.

Lenders often charge points as a way of keeping the stated interest rate down, while increasing their yields. For example, a mortgage with a 6.5 percent interest rate and two points charged to the borrower may be roughly equal to a 6.87 percent mortgage with no points to the borrower.

TIP

You can often trade points against interest rate. If you want a lower monthly payment, you can pay more points up front to reduce your interest rate and payment. If you are short of cash, you can pay fewer (or no) points up front and get a higher interest rate, with higher payments. These days most lenders are amenable to trading points against the interest rate of a mortgage. Just ask.

What Are Adjustable-Rate Mortgages (ARMs)?

In a fixed-rate loan, the interest rate on the mortgage remains the same for the life of the loan. For example, if you begin at 8 percent on the first month, your final payment on the last month is still based on an interest rate of 8 percent.

With an adjustable-rate mortgage, the interest rate fluctuates according to an index. Some of the indices used include T-bill rates, average of mortgage rates, and interbank rate charges (such as LIBOR). Some indices are stable, others volatile. Check the 20-year performance of the index your mortgage is tied to in order to see if it fits your needs.

Crucial elements include how often (the adjustment period) and how far (the steps) the interest rate can fluctuate. Bigger fluctuations mean bigger changes (up or down) in your mortgage payment. There are frequently interest rate "caps" built into the mortgage, precluding it from going beyond a certain top rate. These caps, however, are often very high, perhaps six to eight points higher than the original mortgage rate.

TRAP

Beware of a "teaser" rate, a very low introductory rate to encourage you to borrow. Typically this rate adjusts upward very quickly, often in a matter of a few months, to current market interest rates or higher.

TRAP

Beware of caps on your monthly payment. This will keep your monthly payment down; however, interest that accrues but is not paid because of a payment cap may be added to your mortgage amount. In other words, your mortgage could grow bigger, instead of smaller (called negative amortization)!

TIP

Adjustable-rate mortgages are valuable because they often offer lower interest rates when market rates are very high. In a low interest rate market, however, you are far better off locking in the interest rate with a fixed-rate mortgage.

What Are Balloon Mortgages?

A balloon mortgage has one payment (usually the last) that is higher than all the others. For example, one of the most popular mortgages on the market today is a conforming loan amortized over 30 years (360 equal payments) with a balloon at year 5, 7, or 10.

In other words, you make payments as if you had a 30-year loan. However, instead, it all comes due within a much shorter time. That last, big payment is the balloon. To encourage you to take out this type of loan, lenders reduce the interest rate charged.

TRAP

If you opt for a balloon mortgage, be sure you understand that you must come up with the money (either by selling the property or by refinancing) when that balloon comes due. That's why it's important to have the mortgage agreement include some sort of "rollover" provision that automatically provides for refinancing when the balloon hits—even if that financing is an ugly, high-interest-rate loan.

Are There Other Types of Mortgages?

There are more types of mortgages than you can shake a stick at.

- *Equity-based.* You can get a mortgage on a home purchase even if you have the worst credit in the world, provided you put up a big enough down payment (typically 35 to 40 percent).

- *Asset-based.*   You can get a very low interest mortgage if you put up cash deposits or other assets.
- *Piggyback.*   You can combine a conforming with a portfolio mortgage to get a lower interest rate.
- *Convertible.*   You can get a mortgage that after a period of time converts from adjustable to fixed rate, or the other way around.

TIP

 The number of different types of mortgages is limited by the imagination alone. For a thorough review of the field, look into my book *Tips and Traps When Mortgage Hunting,* 2d ed., New York: McGraw-Hill, 1998.

15

How to Back Out of the Deal Gracefully

This is an unusual chapter to include in a book about buying, since presumably your goal is to purchase the property, not back out of the deal. However, today's real estate market is highly unpredictable: prices may fall over several years and then soar so quickly that every property receives multiple offers. Also, condos, townhouses, and co-ops offer such a different and unusual lifestyle that opportunities for second thoughts abound. You may enter a transaction only to discover that you feel you've paid too much, or the lifestyle just isn't for you. If that's the case, how do you get out of the deal? What is your escape mechanism?

TRAP

It's important to understand that when you sign a purchase agreement, you've signed a document that's intended to be legally binding. Provided all the conditions of the agreement are met, you've agreed to go through with the purchase. Your "out," therefore, must be framed by those conditions.

Should I Check With My Attorney?

While we will look at the matter of gracefully getting out of the deal from a practical perspective, much of it involves the language of

159

clauses inserted into contracts and their legal interpretation. This is the reason, therefore, that you should always contact a good attorney and have him or her read over and give you advice before signing any real estate purchase agreement.

TIP

Real estate attorneys usually charge $500 to $1000 for this service. It's well worth the expense.

What Should I Do Before I Make an Offer?

You should make every effort to be certain that you really want the property. In an ideal situation, that means that you go back to see the property several times. You establish a good handle on the market by viewing enough properties to know comparable prices. And you become thoroughly familiar with the shared lifestyle experience—perhaps by previously owning a condo, townhouse, or co-op or by renting in such a development.

In the real world, however, chances are you are rushing into the deal in order to be sure other buyers don't beat you out; hence you haven't really viewed the property more than once. Further, you may not have had a chance to check out comparable properties to determine true market values. Finally, perhaps you are only learning about the shared lifestyle experience and aren't fully sure it's for you.

If that's the case, then you really shouldn't make an offer, even if an agent or a developer is encouraging you to act. The problem is that you simply don't have enough information to make an educated decision. Rather, you're flying blind and could be heading for a disaster.

What's the Right Approach?

Before you make any offer, you need to know what you're getting yourself into. Therefore, spend some time investigating the shared ownership lifestyle. At the very least, talk to people who live in condos, townhouses, or co-ops.

TIP

If you don't know any owners, you may literally want to knock on some doors. Tell people you're interested in buying one of the units and want to learn more about the development. Most owners will be happy to fill you in not only on the development itself, but on what's involved in a shared lifestyle.

Then spend some time checking out units. See several dozen in your area so that you know what's available. You should have a good sense of how much condos, townhouses, or co-ops cost per square foot, by area, by age, and by quality of construction before making your first offer.

TIP

If you can't walk into a unit and come very close to correctly guessing the price before you are told (or know for sure that the asking price is too high or too low), you're not ready to buy. Spend more time looking!

If you're still not convinced that the lifestyle is for you, you may want to rent a unit for a few months or more. While that may sound like an extreme measure, keep in mind that if you don't like the situation, it's far easier and less costly to get out from a month-to-month rental agreement than it is to turn around and try to sell off a unit you've just bought.

How Do I Back Out After I've Made an Offer?

When you make an offer, you should know, at the very least, what you're committing to and when and how easily you can get out of the deal. This is especially important if you haven't done all the homework I've described above.

One couple I know had a "slash and burn" approach to buying a townhouse. Janet and Fred entered the market at a time when prices were rapidly moving up and properties received multiple offers as soon as they came onto the market. Given the speed with which properties were selling, there just wasn't time to check out a place thoroughly before making an offer.

So Janet and Fred made offers without seeing the property! That's right. If they heard of a townhouse that was in their price range and area, they simply signed a purchase offer, put up a deposit, and had their agent present it to the seller, often just as the unit hit the market. (Sometimes, if they knew the agent, they made an offer before the property hit the "multiple.")

Like as not, their offer was accepted. Then, they would visit the unit at their leisure to see if it was something they really wanted.

But, you may reasonably be asking, what if Janet and Fred hated the townhouse they had "bought"? Since they were buying in California, they knew that they had a built-in escape clause—an automatic three days to approve the disclosures about the property that the seller was required to give. (Time limits for disclosures vary by state. Check with a good agent in your area.) If Janet and Fred decided against a property, their plan was simply to say they didn't approve of the disclosures. Convinced that sellers always disclose something, they felt they were on pretty safe ground.

Do I encourage such tactics? No. They are unethical at best and could land the buyer in litigation if the seller feels the offer was not sincere. On the other hand, do such tactics work? As a practical matter, they usually do.

How Can I Use the Inspection Clauses to Back Out of the Deal?

The trick with escape clauses is to have them inserted into the purchase agreement *before you sign.* The home inspection clause is included to give you time to inspect the property for defects—and then to back out of the deal if you find any that you can't live with. For example, you discover that the condo is contaminated with radon gas (a naturally occurring gas that "leaks" into homes in certain areas of the country). The seller offers to have the gas removed and to install a system to prevent its returning. At this point, you're scared of the gas and just don't want the property any more. A properly drawn home inspection clause should quickly and easily get you out of the deal.

What is a properly drawn inspection clause? It will contain wording that says you have a period of time, typically 10 to 21 days, to have the property inspected by anyone of your choice. Further, in order for the purchase deal to continue, you must give approval to the inspection report. (See Chapter 13 for more information on home inspections.)

TIP

You can approve an inspection report in one of two ways. Either you can actively sign a statement saying you approve it or you can passively fail to notify the seller that you disapprove—meaning you approve it. The method to be used, active or passive, should be spelled out in the purchase agreement.

During the time period you will normally hire an inspector to examine the property and come up with a written report. These reports virtually always list a whole series of things, often quite minor, that are wrong with the property. If you disapprove of the report—and a clause in the purchase agreement gives you the right to back out of the deal upon disapproval—you're off the hook. Usually it's just that simple.

TRAP

Sellers are increasingly wary of buyers who use the inspection report to delay full commitment to the purchase. Savvy sellers are now insisting on an additional clause that says you can get out of the deal only if the report discloses a significant defect, such as a broken foundation or leaking roof. Minor defects, such as cracked tiles, broken screens, or burnt-out light bulbs, do not count. However, this opens the escape clause to interpretation and possible litigation over what's minor and what's major. Check with a good attorney about your rights if you're asked to sign a purchase agreement in which the inspection clause is limited in this way.

What Other Contingencies Can I Use to Exit Gracefully?

A contingency clause in a purchase contract simply says that the purchase is contingent upon or subject to the performance (or lack of performance) of some act. For this reason it is also commonly referred to as a "subject to" clause.

One builder I know insisted that every contract he signed contain at least one "subject to" clause. His feeling was that as long as that clause was in, he could use it to back out of the deal, if he needed to. It's not quite that simple, but the contingency can be effective.

Here are some typical contingencies that can be inserted into purchase agreements:

Sale-of-Home Contingency. You can make the home you're buying contingent upon the sale of your old home. In other words, you don't have to buy the new place until the old place sells. This allows you to tie up a property until you've sold your existing home.

But, you may reasonably ask, why would a seller agree to such a contingency? In a weak market where the seller hasn't had any offers in months, such an offer may seem better than nothing at all. And if you've actually got a buyer and the house you're selling is in escrow, it's not really that bad an offer and could be accepted even in a strong market.

Mortgage Contingency. You can tie the purchase agreement to your ability to get a mortgage (usually specified as to type, maximum interest rate, and maximum points). If the mortgage falls through, you're not required to complete the deal. You may be required to show, however, that you've applied for the mortgage and actually been turned down by the lender.

Relocation Contingency. You can make the purchase contingent on your relocating to the area. If your employer suddenly decides not to relocate you, you're out. But you may be required to show that your employer intended to relocate you and then changed its plans.

Funds Contingency. You can tie the deal not only to your ability to raise funds but also to your ability to obtain a specific amount. For example, you must be able to sell your stock or cash in other assets for a minimum price; otherwise the deal falls through. However, you may be required to show that you actually have funds that can be made available.

Of course, you can make the purchase contingent upon virtually anything. You may insert a clause saying that you won't be required to purchase if there are sunspots during the escrow period, or if hostilities break out in the Middle East, or if your daughter fails to make the soccer team. The contingency protects you and lets you get out of the deal gracefully.

Can an Escape Clause Ever Backfire?

It could. The problem is that contingencies cut both ways. If the seller decides (perhaps rightly so) that your contingencies are frivolous, he or she may simply strike them out, refusing to sign unless they are removed. You've got no deal unless you give up your escape contingencies.

Even if the seller doesn't strike them out, he or she may limit them—for example, by giving you only five days to comply. You don't remove the contingency within five days and now the seller doesn't have to go through with the deal.

The art of an escape contingency is to make it sufficiently believable that the seller will be convinced you are sincere and will go along with you. Dorothy's story is a case in point.

After her grandmother died, Dorothy stood to inherit a considerable amount of money. However, the money was tied up in probate. Yet Dorothy wanted to buy a home quickly, before prices moved up even more than they already had. So she inserted a contingency that the sale could not be completed until probate released funds to her.

The seller became suspicious and contacted the executor of the estate, who indicated that Dorothy did indeed have sufficient funds to make the purchase and that in his estimation it would be no more than 45 days until they were released. So the seller signed—on the contingency that the funds had to be released within 45 days or the sale was off.

As it turned out, the executor of the estate was a close cousin of Dorothy's, happy to release the funds whenever she wished. In other words, Dorothy now had 45 days to make up her mind about the purchase. If she wanted to go through with it, she simply told her cousin to release the funds. If she didn't, she told her cousin not to.

Such an arrangement is definitely not kosher, and could backfire if the seller finds out. But it does illustrate the power of the contingency clause.

What Happens After All the Escape Clauses Have Been Removed?

Sometimes it turns out that just as you're ready to close the deal, after you've removed all the escape clauses, you discover that for whatever reason you don't want to go through with the purchase. Can you still get out of the deal gracefully?

Yes and no. A lot depends on your reason for wanting to get out—and on the seller.

For example, you or a close relative could have a medical emergency, perhaps a stroke or heart attack. Yes, you're committed to making the purchase, but now you have other concerns. You explain the problem to the seller. In such a situation I've never known sellers to refuse to let buyers out of the deal, even in many cases going so far as giving the buyers back their deposit.

On the other hand, perhaps you've found some other condo, townhouse, or co-op that you think is a better deal. You simply want out of your purchase agreement in order to buy another property. Or perhaps you just decide that you don't want to purchase into a shared living development. Or you just don't want to purchase at all. Can you get out?

You could simply refuse to sign the final papers. You could refuse to complete the deal. However, if you do so the sellers would undoubtedly be entitled to keep the deposit. Further, they could take you to court and sue for "specific performance," requiring you to complete the deal.

As a practical matter, sellers rarely try to force buyers to complete a purchase. Usually they just take the deposit and then try to resell to someone else. But you never know how angry your sellers might be and to what lengths they might go.

TIP

If both you and the sellers signed a "liquidated damages" clause, you've probably agreed to lose the deposit as the full damages if you fail to go through with the deal. The seller has agreed not to sue for specific performance in that case. However, such clauses are not always airtight. Be sure you check with a good attorney before signing one and relying upon it.

It is for the above reason that buyers usually try to put up as little a deposit as possible. If they have to back out of the deal and are required to forfeit it, the less money involved the better.

On the other hand, it is for the same reason that sellers try to get the buyers to put up as big a deposit as possible. The more money involved, the sellers correctly reason, the less likely the buyers are to back out.

TRAP

Don't count on the "final walk-through" as a way to back out of the deal. This walk-through is designed to let you see the property one last time just before escrow closes—primarily to assure you that it's in the same condition it was when you first made the offer (that the sellers haven't damaged it in the interim). Usually the final walk-through clause specifies that significant damage must have occurred since you first saw the property. Unless there's a lot of new damage (holes in the walls, broken windows and doors and other damage), you probably won't be able to use this as an escape clause.

16

Bring Your Checkbook to the Closing

If you get your financing, if the seller clears title to the condo or townhouse, if the board approves your purchase of the co-op, if all the necessary documents are in place, if everything that needs to be done gets done, then and only then are you ready to close the deal. Typically the closing takes place at the escrow company or in an attorney's office. You'll come in, sign the necessary documents, and write out checks for all sorts of things.

Write checks? If this is your first real estate transaction, you may be puzzled. After all, you're coming up with a down payment and you're getting financing. What are all the rest of the checks for?

The answer is they are for the myriad other costs that are involved in closing the transaction. These are the infamous closing costs and the fees associated with the mortgage that you're getting. (Pay cash and you can avoid thousands of dollars in fees!)

TIP

Be sure to ask the escrow officer or attorney closing the transaction what form the down payment should be in. Many times only a certified check or an electronic transfer will be accepted. Even on a certified check, there may be a few days' hold. For smaller closing costs, often your check on a local bank will be accepted, particularly if it's going to be several days before escrow actually closes and there's time to have your checks cleared.

What Extra Costs Will I Have to Pay?

As the purchaser, you'll be required to pay many costs, some reasonable, some not. Here's a brief look at what you can expect to pay and why. Note that the list is far from complete. Many more fees may be added for a wide variety of services.

TIP

If this is your first real estate transaction or if you're not thoroughly familiar with how deals are closed, bring an expert with you. It may be your agent, or attorney, or financial adviser. Just make sure your consultant knows real estate closings.

TRAP

These days many real estate agents, particularly good ones, are hesitant to show up with you at closings. Their reason is that you may ask for legal advice, and as an agent who is not an attorney, they are not allowed to provide it. This is a good reason to have an attorney with you at closings. (On occasion I have favored the judgment of experienced real estate agents over that of attorneys who were not intimately familiar with real estate transactions.)

Application Fee

A fee for filling out a loan application? This charge is ridiculous. If you see it, you know you are being asked to pay garbage fees.

Association or Corporation Document Fees

This is a fee to the homeowners association or to the board of directors of the corporation for providing you with documents such as the CC&Rs, the bylaws, and the rules. The charge could be $100 or more. While you may wish the documents were provided free, the association or board can legitimately charge for the service.

Advance Assessment

The homeowners association or the board may require that you pay several months' worth (or more) of dues or fees in advance. If this is the policy, you'll be hard pressed not to pay.

Buyer's Agent's Fee

If you have an agent, this is the fee. However, very often the buyer's agent can negotiate with the seller and the seller's agent over fees. Be sure you bring this up early on.

Buyer's Attorney's Fee

If you have an attorney, this is the cost. It's typically under $1000 and in some cases may be under $500.

Buyer's Escrow Fee

The escrow charges are usually paid by the buyer or the seller, or split by both. If you pay all or some, this is your cost. Check with the escrow company early on to find out what it charges. You may want to shop around for a lower fee.

Lender's Attorney's Fee

If the lender uses an attorney to check over its documents, this is the charge to you. It comes under the heading of a garbage fee. You should never be asked to pay for the lender's attorney. It should be a cost of doing business for the lender. Shop elsewhere if you learn early on that you will be charged for this.

Lender's Escrow Fee

The lender will often run a separate escrow from the one you are running to purchase the home. The cost will be about a third to a half of your escrow fee. This is a semi-garbage fee. The lender may truly need to run the escrow, but the question becomes: Is it the lender's expense or yours?

Origination Fee

This is a charge to you for processing the mortgage. Unless you're getting an FHA loan, it is usually a garbage fee. Yes, there is a cost to the lender, but once again it's a direct cost of doing business and shouldn't be charged to you.

Prorations

This is your share of taxes, insurance, and any other recurring costs prepaid by the sellers. You're simply returning to the sellers the money they paid in advance (for taxes and insurance that go into effect after you take over the property). It's a legitimate charge and you need to pay it.

Recording Fee

This is a pass-through fee. The state or county charges the escrow company and it passes the fee along to you.

Tie-in Escrow Fee

This is a charge by the escrow company for tieing in the lender's escrow to your purchase escrow. If both are run by the same company, it's a garbage fee. On the other hand, if you're selling your old house and tie its escrow into the one on the house you're purchasing, it could be a legitimate fee. It may also be reasonable if two separate escrow companies are involved.

Title Insurance Fee

Title insurance is usually paid by the buyer or the seller, or split by both, according to local custom. If you pay all or some, this is your cost. Check with the title insurance company early on to find out what it charges. You may want to shop around for a lower fee.

Underwriting Fee

This is a fee charged by the lender for processing your mortgage through an underwriter, usually Fannie Mae or Freddie Mac. The charge, typically around $100, should be a cost of doing business for the lender. It's strictly a garbage fee.

Warehousing Fee

The lender will charge a fee for "storing" your mortgage money until you actually need it to close your deal. It's usually a couple of days' interest on the mortgage. This is a deep garbage fee. These days, with electronic transfers, there's no reason the lender should need to warehouse money. And if it does, it can always store it in an interest-bearing account.

Remember, this is just a sampling of the many fees and charges you may be asked to pay.

What If I Don't Want to Pay the Fee?

If you're at closing and no error has been made in addition or subtraction, you're probably stuck. The time to protest the fee is when you hire the lender, the escrow company, the title insurance company, the attorney, or the agent. At the closing, it's usually too late to back out.

TRAP

If you don't like the fees the lender is imposing and decide at the closing to get a different lender, you're pushing your luck. It takes time to get a new lender, and the seller won't be anxious to give you that extra time. You could lose the deal, your deposit, or worse, depending on how the purchase agreement was written.

As noted earlier, when you apply for the mortgage, the lender is supposed to provide you with a detailed estimate of costs under RESPA (the Real Estate Settlement Procedures Act). Read the estimate carefully. It may not contain all the costs, but it will probably list most of them. If there are some you don't understand, or understand and don't want to pay, complain then. If the lender refuses to remove them, you can act with your feet, by going to another lender. As noted, it's usually too late to do that at closing.

The same holds true with the fees for agents, attorneys, escrow companies, and title insurance companies. Ask up front what their fees will be and go elsewhere if you don't like what you hear.

TRAP

There's no guarantee that another lender, agent, escrow company, or title company will have lower fees, but it might. It's certainly worth a look when you're shopping around for them.

When an Owner Defies the Board

The thrust of this book has been on problems that you as an owner may face in dealing with the rules imposed by a condo, townhouse, or co-op board: How might those rules restrict you from doing what you want? But there's another side to this story: What happens when you're on the side of the board? How does the board persuade a group of disparate, single-minded owners to live with and by the rules?

Why Would a Member Go Against the Board?

What if an owner defies the board? What can the board do about it and how will it affect other owners? Checking out this perspective is useful not only for existing owners, but for buyers who are contemplating a purchase decision.

There can be countless reasons for going against the board. As we've already seen, an owner may want to make physical changes that run counter to the rules, bylaws, or even CC&Rs. Or the owner may not like a rule regarding noise or parking facilities or use of the swimming pool. Or the owner may not want, or be able, to pay monthly dues.

When this happens, you as one of the other owners, count on the board to enforce the rules. You want the board to make sure that the stability, security, and investment potential of the development are maintained. You want the board to act decisively to protect your interests.

Why Would the Board Not Be Able to Act?

Again, there are many reasons for a board's failure to act. As a board member of long standing, I can tell you about a few.

- *The board is divided.* Some members want to enforce the rule; others feel that an exception ought to be made. A deadlock ensues.
- *The rules are poorly defined.* The bylaws or even the CC&Rs may be unclear.
- *The board doesn't have the authority.* Poorly drawn bylaws or CC&Rs may restrict the board from enforcing its own rules.
- *There is the threat of recall.* The affected owner may be threatening a recall of the board if it enforces its own policy and the board members may be afraid to act.
- *There is the threat of lawsuit.* If the owner sues, the board may have to defend in expensive litigation.
- *The disputed rule just can't be enforced.* The board doesn't have clear means at its disposal to enforce the rule.

There are lots of reasons the board may fail to act to preserve the integrity of the development. In actual practice, I've seen boards take *some* action more often than not. But that action isn't always wise and sometimes produces unexpected and unwanted results. And there are times when taking action can lead to even more serious problems. Let's consider several different examples.

When the Owner Doesn't Maintain the Premises

In townhouse developments in particular (and in some condos and co-ops), individual owners will have responsibility for some small exterior maintenance. It may be something as simple as keeping their door clean or as complex as maintaining a portion of the lawn in front of their unit. Regardless of the circumstances, what happens when owners refuse to maintain an area that is their responsibility? What can the board do?

One homeowners association wrestled with the problem of a small, unattended lawn in front of an owner's unit. The owner refused to maintain the area and it went to seed, drawing down the appearance of the entire complex.

This was not a new problem for the board; all the owners had the same requirement, and over the years more than one had let the lawn area go. In the past, however, written warnings and eventually fines had always worked to correct the situation.

This time, however, the owner simply ignored the repeated cajoling and threats from the board. She was an attorney and refused to heed the board's call.

After a number of fines had been assessed and not paid, the board was at its wit's end. What could it do now? The board was reluctant to go to court because of the costs involved.

So one day the board authorized a gardening/landscaping service to put in a new lawn and other landscaping. The board also saw to the watering and care of the area. Then it billed the costs to the owner, along with a stiff administrative fee. The board threatened to take the owner to small claims court to recoup the money.

The overall cost was quite high, and it soon became apparent to the owner that having the board take care of her property was far more expensive than doing it herself.

Therefore, she complied. She paid off the past-due costs and continued to maintain her property. This set a precedent for others in the development who might have considered holding back on their maintenance work.

In this case the board took a "self-help" approach. Sometimes it works; sometimes it can have unexpected and undesirable consequences. For example, what if the owner tripped and fell over a tool or plant while the new lawn was being installed—and then held the board responsible? Unlikely, but it could happen. That's why boards should never take self-help action without the considered advice of their attorney.

TRAP

Any good board, no matter how small the development, will have an attorney on call to help in controversial matters. It goes without saying that legal advice for the board is mandatory. Beware of a board that takes self-help measures without such advice.

When the Owner Has Loud Parties

A friend of mine bought into a condo where there were only 15 units. Shortly after he bought in, another unit on the same floor was sold to a couple who loved to have parties.

Although the building had a rule about noise after 10 p.m., the new owners would party until two and three in the morning, particularly on weekends. And during the week they would often play their stereo at an extremely high level, enough to disturb other owners nearby.

Needless to say, my friend and others complained to the board, which immediately asked the new owners to tone it down. They did, for a few days, and then the decibel level went right back up.

The general manager called on them again, and again. Letters of complaint were issued. Fines were assessed. All to no avail. The owners refused to tone down the sound.

What could the board do? Again, the fines couldn't be unreasonably high, and so they were but a thorn in the side of the owners.

TRAP

It's extremely difficult to enforce restrictions on noise. What's very loud up close will not be loud at some distance. Also, even up close, what one person finds loud another will find acceptable. Remember, hearing abilities differ markedly across the population. Decibel counters can be used to provide a scientific basis for the amount of noise, but then it becomes a matter of what decibel level to accept and how close others are to the origin of the sound. These are some small, "good neighbor" concerns that can turn into cans of worms.

Further, unlike the previous situation, no self-help solution was readily available. The board discussed cutting off electricity to the unit, going in and unplugging or breaking the stereo, and even more drastic measures. The condo attorney quashed all such possible actions as being unreasonable and, very likely, illegal. So what could the board do?

TIP

The dilemma of the board is caused in part by the nature of the development. A condo owner has title to the property. The board has limited power in regulating a titled owner. It would be considerably different if the situation were a co-op where the stock owner had a lease. The board could then argue that the owner was violating a condition of the lease by making excessive noise and take immediate action as against a "tenant."

Eventually, the board made the owners an offer they couldn't refuse. The board bought them out at a price higher than the market value of their property. Strange as it may seem, the owners of the condo actually profited from their nastiness!

The board then proposed that the development convert to co-op status. It pointed out that as a co-op board, it could have taken action quicker, cheaper, and more effectively. However, *all* the owners had to agree before such a change could be made. Several owners argued that even though control was better in a co-op, reselling was more difficult because of problems in getting financing (at least in the area where this occurred); thus valuations could be affected. Ultimately, with not all owners agreeing, no change in status was made and the board resold the condo unit, hoping for the best with the new owners.

When the Owner Makes Unauthorized Changes

Unauthorized changes probably pose the most serious problems for a board. While, in general, it's OK to make changes within a unit, those changes must not affect other units and owners. Changes outside a unit, obviously, cannot be made without board approval.

In one condo development where I participated on the board, a homeowner arbitrarily repainted the front of the unit bright blue.

He didn't ask permission, didn't seek advice from anyone. One morning the rest of us woke up to one bright blue unit.

Needless to say the board immediately called a meeting, and several of us went to talk to the owner. We quietly explained that it was against the rules to paint the exterior of an individual unit any color other than the color approved for the whole development. In any event, it was the board's responsibility to take care of painting, not the individual unit's owner.

The owner said he simply wasn't aware of this. But he liked blue and intended keeping it. So it was a standoff. The board's attorney suggested a threat of legal action. She prepared a letter to the owner explaining the board's position and pointing out that if the owner did not comply, the board was determined to take the matter to court. She suggested that the owner consult with his own attorney.

As it turned out, the owner did just that. When he found out what it would cost him to defend in such a lawsuit, he agreed to let the board have the unit repainted the accepted color—and to pay for the cost of repainting.

All of which is to say that sometimes legal action (or the threat of it) can produce the desired results.

TRAP

 Any board that regularly resorts to the threat of a lawsuit to enforce the rules either is acting too hastily or has overly strict rules that are difficult to enforce. The costs of moving in this direction are not cheap for the board or the homeowners it represents.

When the Owner Doesn't Pay Dues

This should be a slam dunk. In a co-op situation, when the owner doesn't pay, the board can quickly (often in a matter of weeks) evict the "tenant" and resell the stock to someone who will pay. In a condo situation, the board can place a lien on the property and go to court to force sale to recoup the money.

But what if it's a situation where the owner is willing to pay, but simply can't?

A friend of mine was a tenant/owner in a co-op when one of the other owners, whom we'll call Peter, was stricken with cancer. Peter had to have surgery, followed by a long recovery period with radiation and chemotherapy, and needed to have a quiet place to recuperate. His co-op unit was the obvious answer.

But Peter, like millions of others in our country, didn't have health insurance. Thus all his available financial resources went to medical treatment. And, of course, he couldn't work. In short, Peter could no longer afford to make the monthly payments. But he couldn't really hope to get well unless he had a decent place to live. (He had no relatives able to step in to help out.)

The board could easily have forced Peter out of the unit (he was hardly in a position to put up strenuous resistance), but then he would have been literally out in the street. And he had lived in the co-op for many years and was friendly with a good many of the owners.

So, taking this as a special case, particularly when other owners came to a meeting to speak up for Peter, the board decided to let things ride for a few months. The board made up Peter's dues from an emergency fund.

TRAP

Emergency funds, unlike other reserves, are designed to be spent each year. However, they are usually designated for specific emergencies, such as snow removal. They can on occasion be used to make up the proportional mortgage and tax payments from an owner who doesn't pay, but usually only on a short-term basis.

After three months, the board took up the matter again. Although improving, Peter was still convalescing, couldn't work, and had no immediate hope of keeping up his dues, let alone paying back what monies the board had already advanced. Again the board considered removing Peter from his unit. And again the other owners, even more this time, came to his defense. Once more the board let him stay.

Overall, Peter remained in his unit nearly a year and a half before he was sufficiently recovered to be able to work. During that entire

time, his co-op dues were paid, in effect, by his neighbors. He stayed
on thanks to their concern and generosity.

Eventually, when he got back on his feet and returned to regular
employment, Peter began making dues payments and also began
paying back the amount the board had advanced him during his illness. Last I heard, he had repaid almost all of the money.

The True Meaning of Community

In this closing segment we've discussed many of the problems and
difficulties that owners have with boards and bylaws and rules. And
we've talked about problems that boards have with individual owners
who bend and break the rules. When all is said and done, however,
it's important to understand that sometimes a shared ownership
development can achieve what few rental or single-family environ-
ments dare aspire to: it can come together as a community.

This is one of the seldom lauded benefits of shared living: a sense
of belonging, of people taking care of their neighbors. In some
respects it's like the "old-fashioned" concept of a self-sustaining village in which every member helps every other. Of course, it doesn't
always happen the way it did with Peter, or at least not in such a dramatic fashion. (People in shared ownership developments do frequently watch each other's homes, meet together recreationally, and
even help out with meals when someone is sick.)

But it is worth remembering that one important part of the rationale behind developing condos, townhouses, and co-ops (besides
getting into an area for less money!) is the village concept. It's an
idea for the millennium.

Index

About the Author

Robert Irwin, noted real estate broker for more than three decades and the author of the best-selling *Tips & Traps* real estate series, serves as a consultant to lenders, investors, and brokers. With over 30 books, including *Buying a Home on the Internet* and *The Pocket Guide for Home Buyers*, Irwin is recognized as one of the most knowledgeable writers in the real estate field.